Servant
of the
Light

ALICE ARMSTRONG WARD
with
A. DUDLEY WARD

tidings

1908 Grand Avenue
Nashville, Tennessee 37203

Library of Congress Catalog Card Number: 72-86490
© 1972 by TIDINGS, 1908 Grand Avenue
Nashville, Tennessee 37203
All rights reserved
E205B

CONTENTS

INTRODUCTION

Alice Ward was a very beautiful person. It is important to understand this because someone reading this book without having known her personally might think she was some kind of "freak." There is no doubt that she had unusual spiritual powers, but she was first of all a beautiful person.

She loved her husband, her children, and her home and poured herself into her life as wife and mother. She surrounded herself and her family with beauty—flowers, music, and good books—and with things which contribute to health—nutritious food, a relaxed atmosphere, and a deep love for persons and for God's world. And who of us who knew her will ever forget her delightful sense of humor! With dancing eyes she would laugh with us at humorous situations which we hadn't even noticed until she revealed them to us.

She also loved the church. Regular participation in the prayer life and worship of the church was as important to her as breathing! Weekly communion was a source of great refreshment to her. But there was more. Unlike many of us who are so eager to "reform" the church by destroying the organization, she clearly saw the need for healthy organizational structures and she gave of herself by attending board meetings and conferences and by encouraging us when we became discouraged with the weight of the ecclesiastical superstructure. How many times, also, when we were building our ministry of healing she counselled us to keep it in the main stream of the church's life. Now I see clearly the wisdom of her words.

It is very important to understand this emphasis in her life. Too many persons with the kind of gift she possessed leave the church or are asked to leave the church. Even though the Bible is filled with the experiences of spiritually sensitive persons, the church has felt uneasy and has tended to isolate itself from all this. But Alice clearly viewed her spiritual sensitivity as a gift from God to be used within the context of God's community. She taught us that God's presence within the community of faith enhances the value of spiritual gifts and prevents their misuse.

This is a lesson which is urgently needed in a time when many people are turning away from the church in a search for "relevance," only to find themselves caught up in the often destructive sensationalism of psychic phenomena. Alice's gift was especially valuable because she insisted that it be experienced, examined, and confirmed within the community of faith. We would be wise to follow her guidance and her example.

Alice Ward was also a "servant" in the purest sense. She cared deeply about people and freely gave of herself in order to help them find wholeness of life. She exercised her healing gift in many different ways, always sensing what was "right" in any given situation. She never used her gift to exploit others or impress others, but always to help them find wholeness of life. Countless hours were often spent in helping one person find the light. And toward the end, when her own strength was failing, she continued to care and to give freely of herself in helping those who turned to her in suffering and pain.

Most important, Alice was a woman of prayer. Her deepening union with God was the source of her power, of her insight, of her love. It is so important to understand this "secret" about Alice. I do not believe she would want this book published if it did no more than show what a gifted person she was. But if it convinces us that we all have spiritual gifts and that prayer can bring them forth in each of us, then she would be happy, for this is what she tried to tell us, over and over again.

I can still remember one of the ministers at her memorial service saying, "Alice Ward was a no nonsense girl!" When it came to the disciplines of prayer and meditation she stood for no nonsense, no flimsy excuses, no laziness, and no short cuts. I have never known anyone who worked harder or longer on learning to pray. She believed there are "laws" of prayer just as there are laws of nature and she was determined to discover them. She had little patience with those who wanted to enjoy the fruits of the spiritual life without obeying the laws.

Because of the prayer foundation on which she built her life, her spiritual gift increased in its power to heal and in the depths of its love. I am now positively convinced that those of us who are unwilling to take upon ourselves the spiritual and physical disciplines of prayer and meditation and do the hard work involved in learning the laws of the spiritual life have no right to dismiss Alice Ward's gift lightly. Even if we choose to go on living in the dark we can rejoice in knowing one who attained the freedom and joy of living in the light of God's love.

The greatest value of this book is in the opportunity it provides each one of us to confront the reality of prayer and meditation in our lives in a new way. If we will discipline ourselves and learn to pray, then God will call forth our gifts, and we will become, in our own ways, servants of the light.

—Edward W. Bauman
Senior Pastor
Foundry United Methodist Church
Washington, D.C.

AUTHOR'S PREFACE

The search for spiritual vitality and sensitivity is an unusual and rewarding experience for anyone who will honestly develop and maintain the disciplines required. Certain persons have natural gifts which facilitate their search and development. But whether or not endowed with special capacities, each person can find an increasing awareness of God and his spirit.

This book shares the life experiences of Alice Ward, one who did have special gifts and sensitivities, unrecognized for many years. Through personal discipline and a diligent search for expanding life in the Spirit, Alice became a truly whole person in the midst of a nearly twenty-year struggle with cancer, which finally took her life on March 15, 1969. Many of the circumstances and the family context of her life and struggle with cancer are related in the book, *I Remain Unvanquished,* published in 1970.

Each of the following chapters contains illustrations of Alice's special gifts and sensitivity. They indicate the wide range of persons and events which contributed to her growth. They are not presented in any chronological sequence, but rather as separate life-segments that she experienced and about which she wrote.

All the illustrations have special meaning and credibility. They are all about real people, most of whom are still living. While the illustrations include few individual names, I know, have identified, and have recorded all the names. The persons involved also can attest to the events.

I make no claims that all persons can experience the same type of events or that generalizations can be made which apply to all people. I do believe that each person can become increasingly sensitized to the wider ranges of spiritual experience. In the usual routine of life we cannot readily comprehend many of the details recorded here. But I am firmly convinced that they did and will continue to happen.

I hope this book will encourage its readers to take a "leap of faith" into the wider reaches of spiritual growth. The biblical record, church history, and individual religious experiences down through the ages testify to the fact of unlimited possibilities for all persons. The church and the religious community have known aspects of these wider ranges. Many individuals have known them.

However, the church has been hesitant to use and proclaim these possibilities. It is time for the church and its people to move beyond the narrow confines of a rigid approach to spiritual life and to venture into these areas which are distinctly a part of her heritage. The credibility of the search has never been as high as both physical and psychological sciences reveal depths and ranges of human nature for new life in dimensions beyond the generally accepted physical, psychological, and spiritual limits.

While I make only minimal claims for the particular events presented in the chapters of this book, I hope they will open for readers new possibilities for courage, zest, and activity into the wider realms of spiritual growth. May God bless you as you read, contemplate, and begin to move out with him.

—A. D. WARD

I
BEGINNINGS—LIFE AND ITS POTENTIAL

INTRODUCTION

What did I come from? What heritage and influences have determined my development and brought changes to my nature and experience? How have I used the qualities inherited and infused?

These and other typically crucial questions confront a person seeking to evaluate the present situation and make some projection for the future. This characteristic of high regard for inheritance and subsequent experience was fundamental to Alice's life. She began to recognize the deep meanings of life as they emerged in her own capacities of sensitivity and for spiritual, emotional development.

The incidents recorded in this chapter are simply selected from many which could have appeared. They combine events which reinforced the awareness that not only did Alice have special endowments, but that their meaning is often best appreciated through very ordinary things: childhood revolt against the will of parents and other adults; awareness that hard work and pride aid in the development of capacities to do lovely things of simple meaning like making a fine horseshoe; recognition that death, especially of someone very close and young, as a part of human existence can become a beautiful memory, a source of wonder and strength in many relationships with others who face tragedy.

Throughout all her life came the slowly increasing awareness that spiritual vitality in a direct encounter with God in Jesus Christ is the bedrock of existence, the source of power that releases potentials often buried deep within the subconscious. The excitement of discovery of this release—the how, when and what—is an unparalleled adventure for each person willing to put the time, energy, and personal discipline into the quest.

A.D.W.

EARLY IMPRESSIONS AND INSIGHT

I grew up in a Canadian home including a real sense of the presence of God and his influence in life, not in any fundamentalist manner, but rather in a deep and living consciousness in the lives of my parents. We were Presbyterian, always attended Sunday school and church regularly, and took an active part in the work of the church. Even at an early age I remember my search to find out more about Jesus and the Christian life. I used to page through many of my father's periodicals and books, particularly his hymn book from which I would memorize verses and search for their meaning, often confused by the words.

To obtain fresh milk in our town one had either to keep a cow or buy from someone who had extra milk to sell. We tried to spare a couple of quarts a day of our cow's milk for others. While it often meant quite a little walk, especially in the winter, to deliver the milk we sold, I insisted on going two places no matter what the weather.

One place was the home of a Catholic couple who were always glad to see me and kept a light in the window to guide me up the lane. After they emptied the milk into their container, they would allow me to go into the parlor where I would sit in silence looking at a picture of Christ. After a long time I got up enough courage to ask the Catholic lady, "When did he send you his picture?" To me Christ always seemed such a real, living person, one who could, if he wished, send his picture to a person.

A second home I visited when delivering the milk had in its parlor a sea shell, something rather unusual in northern Ontario. Each day the lady would let me go into her parlor, take the shell in my hands, and hold it to my right ear. In a few moments it seemed my whole being would vibrate with the sound of the ocean, and I thought it the most beautiful sound in all the universe.

Then a sad day came when the woman told me they were moving away. I remember the feeling of utter despair and my great desire not to be separated from the sound of the sea. How overjoyed I felt when on the final day of packing she called me in and gave to me the sea shell that I have kept ever since.

Much later in my life, during my search, I learned that the

14

highest sound in the universe was the "om" sound and that you would hear it the loudest in your right ear. Of course, it sounded like a waterfall or the movement of the ocean and it brought with it a great sense of unity and peace with the One.

Another incident that impressed me as a young child of about five happened on a day when my mother was combing my hair. I took my mother's hand in mine and startled myself by saying to her, "Oh Mother, you are going to live almost twice as long as Daddy."

She withdrew her hand and said, "You must not say those things, Alice." This troubled me because the thought came to me so suddenly and I knew it was true. But I completely forgot about it until my father died suddenly at forty-nine. Mother lived forty years longer.

A HORSESHOE FROM THE BLACKSMITH SHOP

I received one of the great thrills of my youth by standing in the doorway of my father's blacksmith shop and watching as he shod the horses. He had taken up this trade as a young man, and in this area of the country he had all types of horses brought to him in this era before the use of cars and trucks. He not only shod the horses, but he designed different types of horseshoes to fit the hoofs of the various horses and their particular need, much the same as a shoemaker would make special types of shoes.

During these years, he and his partner kept samples of the various types of horseshoes. As they became more proficient in their trade, they had these sample horseshoes silvered or covered with gold leaf. Gradually they built up quite a collection, and I remember my father's big horseshoe display showing them framed and hanging in his shop. When many years later his garage was destroyed by fire, this valuable and prized collection also got caught in the blaze. However, the iron did not melt, although the silver and gold did.

One of my older brothers gathered and kept these horseshoes through the years. My father's partner lived much longer than he did, and when he retired my brother persuaded him to take the horseshoes and remold them. They then had them silvered and inlaid with gold as they had been originally. None of us knew about this project until the fiftieth wedding anniversary of my father's partner at which time my brother bought the horseshoes for display. We all were thrilled to see them again, and each one felt a little envious, secretly desiring to own one of the horseshoes personally. But we knew that the collection must not be broken up, and it rightfully belonged to our brother.

After coming home from the hospital following a serious illness in 1965, I saw one of these horseshoes with my mind's eye. At first I thought I must be imagining it, and then I knew it appeared so realistically and so often that it couldn't be imagination. I saw it quite distinctly, even the number of nail holes in it. I kept putting it out of my mind because I would not permit myself to think about breaking up the collection. As I kept seeing it, I did have a great desire to hold once again in my hand one of my father's horseshoes as though in some intangible way it would put me in contact with him.

My husband had to go back to Canada during this period. One evening he sat with my brother, and they spoke about me. Suddenly my brother jumped up and went out of the room. In a little while he returned with his hand in his mackinaw. Looking at Dudley, he said, "Here, take this to Alice," and handed him one of the horseshoes.

Dudley knew how much I admired and loved my father, and he realized this would make me very happy. When he returned home and gave me the gift, I immediately looked to count the number of nail holes in the very finely tooled shoe. It was exactly as I had seen it on the wall, three nail holes on the left side, and four on the right side.

This simple horseshoe brought with it a great spiritual blessing. In some way it seemed almost a message from my father of his concern for me and of his presence with me.

THE FIRST EXPERIENCE OF DEATH

The first person I saw die was my sister, Joyce, youngest member of a family of eleven. Never very strong after her birth, when little over a year old she became quite ill with a flu infection that settled in her chest and caused her arms to swell

16

so badly she could not move them without assistance. We took turns helping our mother care for her.

One night as the family was eating supper, a neighbor lady came in to sit with Joyce for awhile and Mother and I went into the room with her. As we stood there looking at the little child in the crib, we suddenly became aware of a light around her head which increased in dimension and brilliance until it filled the entire hood of the crib. Then we watched as the swollen arms began to move from her sides and slowly reached upward as though guided and held by unseen hands. We heard a voice that for days had not uttered a word say in a beautiful tone, "Oh Mama, Mama." At that moment the glory engulfed her entire body. In the next instant the light faded, the arms quietly fell to her side, and the spirit that had become so endeared to all as "our angel" had left the physical body.

VISION OF AND RESPONSE TO CHRIST

On March 13, 1938, a cold winter night in Toronto, I stood waiting for a streetcar that would take me across the city to a church service I had been invited to attend. Entering the sanctuary I did not see my friend, so I sat down among the strangers. The minister spoke of the blessing of growing up in a family where the parents were committed Christians, but he stressed that this in itself was not enough. Every man, individually, had to make his own decision for Christ.

It was several months since my father's sudden and untimely death. He had stood as a symbol for all that was good and Christ-like in my world. As a small child I had known the security of a father's love, had thrilled when I heard him sing, "On Christ the solid rock I stand, all other ground is sinking sand." I knew with surety that he stood on a rock and although I could not comprehend the meaning, I somehow felt that by keeping close to him, I could also be on the rock. Now he was gone and I was seeking to find this needed security in my life and world.

As the congregation sang the last hymn, the spirit of God spoke to me. With each stanza the voice became more persistent and I countered with escape arguments. During the final verse

I was no longer singing, but looking up to the altar, seeing Christ in all his radiance standing there. His hands were outstretched and in a voice that rings as clear in my ears today as it did that night he said, "Alice, won't you come?"

I moved out from where I stood, walked to where Christ stood, placed my hands in his and knelt at his feet. That night I heard the word with conviction, answered his request for my life, saw him face-to-face, and experienced the power of his love flowing through me.

I remember how far distant from what I had experienced were the voices of strangers inquiring of me as though expecting me to tell them some sordid story from which I had been saved. I hurried from the church and rode back across the city, outwardly the same person, but inwardly knowing that I had in truth both seen and touched the Rock of which I had heard my father sing.

II
VISIONS AND VITALITY

INTRODUCTION

The Bible is dotted with stories of visions and revelations to those searching for and listening to God. Some brought words of judgment; others beautiful insights into possibilities quite beyond the expectations of the seeker.

Moses saw God in a burning bush. Abraham saw the promise for a nation living in harmony and joy following the will of God. Isaiah saw the Holy One high and lifted up in the temple. His vision not only brought realization of personal limitations, but of unusual development of the strength and beauty within him. Mary, the mother of our Lord, had a vision of a sacred visitation with the promise of the Saviour to come.

Three disciples saw Jesus transfigured before them. Paul was shaken and remade on the way to Damascus. The entire drama of the Bible culminates in a cosmic panorama which encompasses both time and eternity as John the Divine views the ultimate triumph of the Lord over evil and the realization of a kingdom of qualities beyond all the imagination of human kind. The church throughout its history has known these phenomena in countless ways and on unlimited occasions. Both its simple and mighty have experienced direct visions and revelations on various, diverse, and unusual matters.

On this vast biblical and historical experience, the Christian today, attuned to the Holy Spirit, can have confidence that God will reveal himself directly, clearly, and with guidance. The incidents recorded in this chapter are only a few from the life of one person. The exact meaning is not always known, the circumstances not always the same, the results not always evident in pragmatic terms.

However, one may hold a legitimate expectancy that the modern Christian may also experience such manifestations. And again, it becomes even more credible today as science has produced significant confirmation of unusual visionary experience and the promise of almost unlimited possibilities for the adventure into the future.

Over the years Alice and I shared experiences such as those in this chapter as part of our spiritual search and growth. God spoke to us and we came to know him through joy, both in personal and material ways, the grace of his spirit within, and the blessing of mission in society.

During August 1968, for instance, I began and completed work on a small book for Tidings Press. I sat several nights in our bedroom with Alice, who had a recurrence of her illness. As I waited in the silence, I concentrated on the meaning, scope, and context of the book.

One night an occurrence took place and happened in the same manner for the next two nights. From behind me came a stream of light, as though from a visual projection, and through me flowed a stream of consciousness. This was projected as on a screen which appeared above Alice's head.

On the first night and the two following ones, the entire outline, the detailed content, persons to be discussed, and particularly the concluding section on renewal and mission, including the specific reference sources, appeared clearly on the screen. During the entire procedure Alice slept peacefully and I watched in raptured silence. Each time, after the appearance of one section, the light faded and the screen disappeared.

Several years earlier, Alice called me early in the morning when I was in Chicago during particularly difficult and energy-consuming experiences in my work. She read me a vision which she had had and after the call immediately mailed me the piece of paper on which she had taken it down as it came to her:

It was like being on a plateau, not conscious of seeing oneself in it. I did not see myself. The figures did not appear to be people, but indistinct kinds of similar figures, some more distinct than others. The predominant color was bluish turquoise. Some had white spots in the blue which gave a polka-dot effect.

One of the amazing things was that some of them had the facility to move out with great ease from the plateau into space. None were tied rigidly or bound hard. There was much movement, no unhappiness, no rigidity, some did not move from the plateau but this did not appear to be due to any anchor or restriction. They were a company, always together, some moved into the atmosphere freely, others did not.

Very beautiful, lovely experience. The awareness lasted a long time even after I awakened. There was no sense of time, space, or location, just complete sense of life, happiness, and right relationships. The background had a rosy hue to it.

Our interpretation of the vision gave me inspiration, hope, peace, confidence, and energy. The indistinct figures meant that no person or group was threatening me or the work of the Board or the church. All the people involved were free to move with ease into all the possibilities open to them—and so was I! There would be no arbitrary restrictions, no ill will, no hurt feelings, nothing but vital life.

The bluish-turquoise color was always present in Alice's visions when the Holy Spirit was present and working. The rosy hue of the background signified the glory of God. This was one of many such enriching experiences that Alice and I shared.   —A. D. W.

SPIRITUAL AWAKENING
AND A CHILD'S GREAT SOUL

During the coffee hour following the morning worship service at Foundry United Methodist Church in Washington, D. C., I first met Mark. His wife came up and introduced herself, then said, "I would like you to meet my husband." As I turned to greet him, I instantaneously saw both the greatness and desperate need of this man's soul, like seeing a double exposure. I felt the impact so much I could hardly keep up a normal flow of courtesies. When I came home I spoke to my husband about the encounter, since the man had been in the class my husband conducted. During this experience my husband had seen Mark literally coming alive.

I had no occasion to meet this man again for several weeks. But I became aware that during several nights a girl about ten years old was bringing him, by the hand, to the side of my bed and asking me to pray for him. A small red birthmark on the left side of her face identified this child in the spirit to me.

After a time I inquired about their family and learned they had two children, a son, six, and a daughter, eight. Upon further inquiry I discovered they also had a retarded child away at school—a daughter ten years of age. I knew this child brought her father to me for help. A few weeks later he asked to come to talk with me. Out of that encounter and other subsequent events, a new spiritual awareness began to develop.

At this time an answer to prayer came in the formation of a men's prayer group at Foundry Church. I invited Mark to become a participant. Reluctantly he joined, and soon became a very apt student. He grew so that in a year's time when I relinquished leadership of the group, he became the leader.

The first time his eldest daughter came home he brought her to see me. She had a red birthmark on the left side of her face and the father was amazed at the immediate identification that existed between us, and at the warmth of our greeting.

As we met, this retarded child did something that astounded her father and gave to me further insight into my former life. After she had affectionately embraced me, she stepped back and did a beautiful curtsy. Her father exclaimed, "Camille, who taught you to do that?"

"No one, Daddy, I only do it because I am meeting Alice Ward."

One Sunday when the three of us were talking in the chapel of the church, saying goodbye as she was returning to her school, Camille took my hand and said, "Goodbye, servant."

Her father said, "Oh, Camille, you never speak to Mrs. Ward in that way."

"Yes," she said, "Mrs. Ward is a servant, Daddy." The confirmation came as it had come previously that this body contained a great soul, one whom I had known before and who knew my true person now.

Grace continued to work in the lives of this man and his family. When a change came in his government position, he sought guidance, and the entire transition that followed occurred in confidence and joy. All members of the family received a blessing and benefit.

THE ALLNESS OF THE LIGHT

On one Monday morning in 1966 I finished my ironing and went into the library to mend. It was the usual time for my meditation, but a very unusual thing happened, very quickly in the space of a few moments in earth time.

Suddenly I felt the presence and aliveness of Light around my feet and spreading across the floor. Unbelievably a million, trillion lights moved very quickly upward. I felt that something marvelous was about to happen. The room had not been cleaned after weekend activity. Dust on the face of the television seemed to stand out grain for grain; books were spread all over the desk; records lay out of their jackets; dog hairs showed up on the rug. Certainly the room was in no condition to receive a guest. I had an instant urge to tidy it all up, get out the vacuum, because something wonderful seemed about to happen!

Then, in an instant, I knew I had but one choice—to become a part of the Light. I watched as it streamed through the window in great rays, entering everything—all the books, regardless of their contents or authorship; all the records, jazz, dance, religious, classical. The dog hairs, the dust, the furniture, even the needle in my hand, were penetrated by the vibrations of light. The entire room vibrated and I became completely a part of this great current.

When I regained consciousness, I lay on the floor with no sense of time, yet fully aware of what had taken place. After awhile I received instructions to get up and take nourishment. Two hours had passed by the clock from when I had gone into the room. I had a tremendous feeling of renewed energy within, and a consciousness that all is part of creation. I knew that one can only respond when the Light comes; if a person relates to anything lower, he misses the highest. It comes when the place is right, but not necessarily outwardly perfect or even spotless.

AUTHORITATIVE COMMAND
AND BODILY RESPONSE

During my weeks in the hospital in the fall of 1965 I tried to explain to my doctor and my husband the feeling of need for some specific food. I felt that if I could obtain this food it would save a crisis that could come from a developing imbalance in my system. The doctor did not have anything to suggest for me to use at the time.

My husband had to leave for an important meeting, but offered to go to a nearby fruit store and purchase some fresh fruit for me. He brought back some peaches, pears, and large blue grapes. I decided, once he had left, to wash and eat a few grapes. While I was washing a bunch of these grapes in the sink, my right hand began to twist and turn uncontrollably. At first I tried to control it, but soon realized that I should put the grapes back and call a nurse.

The next thing I knew, I was lying between the wall and the bed. My right arm hung like a string of spaghetti at my side. Since my room door was closed, I knew that somehow I had to get back to the bed and reach the call button. I accomplished this by pushing with my feet and gradually working myself up to the bed with my right arm dangling over the edge. A great surge of strength passed through me and with my left hand I grabbed my right arm and in a voice filled with authority I commanded it in the mighty name of Jesus Christ to live and to respond to the life within it. I felt it tingle and by the time the nurse came, I had managed to get it back on the bed. By the time the house doctor had arrived, life had returned to the arm and I could snap my fingers. The nurse called my physician and my husband who left a staff meeting to come back to the hospital. When they arrived, I described to them in detail what had taken place.

Since then, through the years, the thumb and forefinger have a slight numbness. But I have insisted upon doing intricate tasks —knitting, sewing, painting, gardening, in addition to all the household tasks required. I have not had a similar recurrence and have lived without any stress or strain in this area.

A VISION OF ST. THERESA
In one's own life a person often comes in interesting and unusual ways to meet other people and know them as friends. This often occurs through the unexpected or unique experience.

One night as I knelt in prayer at the altar of our church during a service for healing, I looked up and saw a lady standing before me. She had a most beautiful face, very fine and sensitive, and she wore the habit of a Catholic nun. Her lovely hands, in which she held a white rose, showed me her youth.

I could see the dew on the petals of the rose. Then she made a gesture to give it to me and placed it close to my face, and I smelled the fragrant perfume.

As I looked at the nun in rapture, she said, "My name is Saint Theresa, the little flower of Jesus." Then the vision gradually faded until I could see her no more. I had never heard of her and knew nothing about her.

I came home to search in my library for more information about her. Saint Theresa's life story greatly fascinated me. I felt that I truly began to know and have a new friend in the realm of the Spirit. Many times since then I have felt her presence near me, with the attending blessing and the fragrance of the rose.

She was only one of the many people in the Spirit realm whom I have known through my life time. It seems to me one can discern her rate of vibration and see the auras around her. I find nothing strange about this. It has always been beautiful and normal for me to commune with the saints. They have been my friends. Many times in prayer they appear lifting my prayer request to a higher spirituality, many times taking it from me completely.

There have been a few occasions when I have known sheer ecstasy—times when I have seen the saints gathering in the special place for prayer. In the vision the place appears like a beautiful, glimmering garden, all in dazzling white, and those who come are in radiant white robes. I could feel the vibrant power and flow of energy and was caught up in the wonder of it all.

AN EXPERIENCE IN SPEAKING

For me any speaking experience requires extensive study, research, and prayer about the topic or theme. I have to take precise care in writing, especially about personal references or stories.

In the actual speaking experience I feel an inner command to let go of carefully written notes. I have a sense of emptiness, that often increases, until the moment I get up to speak. Often I'm aware of one or two people who stand in spirit beside me. I have an infilling of the Spirit and the consciousness that another speaks through me. I use all the material I gathered but often in another form and always more beautiful and powerful. I make personal references with an honesty and helpfulness that I could not have possibly created. Always I feel the Spirit working within me and speaking through me.

When I feel the Spirit moving out, I know this is all that really matters. It moves out in beams of Light. I can watch the Light as it comes to a person in the audience. Often it encircles the person and I am tempted to cry out, "Receive it, receive it!" I know that if he would, everyone around him would receive a blessing.

One evening speaking to a group gathered in the sanctuary of an Episcopal church, the Spirit moved in power and a lady in the congregation asked, "If I were to come and touch you, would I become like you in Spirit?"

I explained to her that I had no power to transmit the Light to her, but that it was all around her, and that if she put her hand into the hand of Christ she would receive the power. This she did at that very moment and the Light spread over the assembled group with many blessings.

This often happens when a group or audience remains silent. As I speak I can see the Light spreading without anyone saying anything to interrupt the flow of events.

Other times I watch the Light move in their midst and encircle a person. When the person rejects the Light, he becomes more rigid. Gradually, quietly, it often recedes and then fades from vision, and that person experiences no great blessing.

The mastery of my words is not the standard that is required. I am required to be a good workman. It is the power of the "word" spoken in simplicity and truth by the living presence of Christ through me. I am only a vehicle through which the transmission takes place. During these times of speaking I have great protection from the Spirit.

On one occasion when I was the lone woman facing a male audience, the Lord drew a circle around one man sitting about midway in the group. I was told this man had come with a heavy heart, burdened by a family problem unknown to anyone else. He would ask me many personal questions, but I was not to become disturbed because the Spirit had prepared the answers for me.

During lunch the groups requested the opportunity to ask questions. Soon this man spoke up. As his questions became more probing, the embarrassment of the group increased. To my own great amazement, I answered each question directly, calmly, and with a wisdom far beyond my capacity.

Following the afternoon session and communion, that man came to me with tears on his cheeks and said, "This day has changed my life." Not until months later did any of his fellow ministers know what had prompted the long trip he took to be present that day, nor the burden he had brought with him. I remember it not as just an incident when I saw another man's problem and knew the presence of the Spirit in a situation, but rather as the great love of God reaching out to meet the need of one of his children who was truly seeking help.

III

NEW DIMENSIONS IN SPIRITUAL GUIDANCE

INTRODUCTION

A legitimate question for a person evaluating the material in this or any other record of its kind, is, "What practical purpose and effect can such experiences have?" This book and its companion volume, *I Remain Unvanquished,* witness to the fact that personal enrichment, the capacity to deal with both joys and disasters, immediate access to the power of the Holy Spirit, all result from the disciplined search for spiritual growth and vitality.

One of the most immediate and productive results is the increased capacity to relate to others on deep levels, especially for persons, such as Alice, who have native abilities and special capacities for response to the direction of God's spirit. In her work of counselling many hundreds of people she used a unique procedure.

She did not ask more than a few general questions about age, family, and background. She did encourage freedom of the person to speak, but in a disciplined and pertinent way. In most cases, however, she would, following some introductory questions and response by the person, engage in periods of silence with the visitor participating. Some could sustain the silence for a considerable time, others for only a short period. Out of this silence and meditation, insights into the person's past and present life would emerge as well as isolation of the problem. This might not occur the first time together, but for a serious searcher the insights almost always came.

Her process of therapy was not necessarily the usual pattern, as the illustrations given here indicate. However, to my knowledge, substantiated by the record, those who in disciplined fashion followed the careful, loving guidance and ministry received help, many times miraculously. Alice had an increasing sense of assured guidance in her dealings with people. She carefully avoided situations that required special treatment beyond her own capacities. But complexity never deterred her.

Many requests for prayer came to us from persons in trouble or on behalf of someone else. If not known to us, we would ask the person some questions about the need, the seriousness of the request, and his or her willingness to run the risk of a genuine encounter with God, through prayer power, that might radically affect life. If we noted any hesitation, we invited the person to give serious consideration to the risk involved in being in the stream of prayer power. We often said, "We are not in the eye-dropper prayer business," and urged the person to call back within twenty-four hours. Many, not ready for such eventuality, did not call. This approach is indicative of the guidance which has come through the years in dealing, through spiritual therapy, with the troubled and those seeking fulfillment and new adventures in spiritual growth which would enrich the total life.

—A. D. W.

DIANNE AND HER RING

One of the very interesting and exciting events that happened in the life of our daughter, Dianne, was the buying of a ring on her birthday during her second year in college. Dianne was a petite girl, very dainty, with small feet and delicate hands. When we came to choose the ring for her, I insisted on a large dinner ring, not out of proportion, but much larger than I knew she would normally choose, because, although small physically, she was a big person in herself.

Therefore, I knew she had to wear something to bring out within her this larger self. I felt a beautiful ring would serve this purpose. So we chose for her an amethyst dinner ring and sent it by mail to her at college. We received a phone call in a few days from a very disturbed young girl, not knowing how to thank us and yet tell us in a tactful way that it was absolutely too large for her to wear. It looked strange on her hand, she said, and her friends advised her to have us exchange it for a smaller one.

I replied, "Dianne, don't listen to your friends. Listen to me. We have chosen that ring for a special purpose, because we know that you are a big person yourself, and you have to wear something to remind you constantly of this. Put that beautiful ring on and don't take it off. Wear it to your classes, not for just special occasions. It will remind you and help you affirm within yourself your real selfhood and your destiny as a person in the world."

She followed our advice and fell in love with the ring, seeing in it different beauty each day. It became a symbol to her of her real self. She no longer listened to many of the things her friends would say to her. She began to follow the guidance of the self within her. She found a new strength and a new power, and her whole physical body changed. She became a beautiful woman, not only within herself, but physically. The body itself showed a wonderful coordination of all its parts. She has often remarked to us that the ring did more for her than anything else that she ever possessed, and it happened at a most critical time in her life.

A BROTHER SELLS PROPERTY

One of my brothers owns much virgin timber land in Ontario on the shores of many beautiful lakes. A few years ago he had given me a piece of property on one of the larger lakes on which to build a cottage at some future time. Then he considered selling all the other available land around this lake. This involved a great deal of attention to detail and information regarding the sale of land and taxes and what it could mean to his estate. Dudley went to Canada to interview the tax department in Toronto and to obtain all the information he could.

My brother had two offers for this land, one for cash, the other for a down payment and then subsequent payments over a three-year period. So my brother had real questions about which was the better of the two offers. My husband, a chartered accountant familiar with the laws of Canada, accompanied my brother and helped to advise him in his contact with these two competing purchasers. After getting all the information they could obtain at that time, my husband returned to our home in Washington concerned about how he should guide my brother in his decision on the sale of this land.

I told him not to worry unnecessarily because he wouldn't have to make this decision or even help my brother make it. Other forces at work would guide and direct my brother to make the right decision.

One evening our phone rang. It was my brother calling from Canada to tell me that in spite of the late hour, he knew that he had to make the decision that night. He had known it all day since he had awakened that morning, but had put it off. Now he knew he should not let the day end without making the final decision.

He had decided to sell it to the people who had made the offer for less money and over a three-year period of time. He felt that in the long run he could deal and work with these people with the least strain and more effectively. He wanted to let Dudley know of his decision.

I told him he was right in his decision and that he should complete the transaction as guided that night. "Why are you so sure?" he asked. "You have not been in on it."

"Oh, yes, I have been very much in on it in prayer," I replied, "and, while praying the other morning, our father appeared to me in spirit. He has often appeared so that I wasn't shocked at all to see him standing before me. But I was surprised to see another man with him. When I asked father who was with him, he said, 'Alice, it is my brother.' At the time I did not recall that he had a brother, having not known him in my lifetime. He reminded me that his brother had died in his early twenties, that his progress in the spiritual world had been very phenomenal, and that he was well informed on many of the things that concerned you. He said I shouldn't be anxious any more about this land deal. They were with you, father said, and were giving you the necessary guidance on the sale of this land."

Then I described to my brother exactly how this uncle of ours looked. Named Francis, he had the build of one of our seven brothers, but he also had some very special features that I described in detail. Amazed, my brother said, "You know, of all the members of the family, I am the only one who has a picture of this uncle."

A FAMILY HEALS ITS WOUNDS

I had taken a book with me to our Sunday school class to give to a friend, but she had not come that day. In the course of our class discussion I had referred to the book several times. At the close of our session a woman came to me with desperation in her eyes asking for the loan of the book. Feeling her great need, I gladly gave it to her. This led to a visit from her and the unfolding of a very interesting story.

She had married an officer in the navy, and they had known several years of happiness together. Having had no children of their own, they adopted a little girl. Then tensions and misunderstanding began to develop in their lives. Although her husband had undergone counselling, the tensions increased.

Everything ended she said, one rainy night when he had gone out, taken the car, and driven off. Later a telephone call informed her that an accident had occurred and her husband was in the hospital unconscious. Later his physicians moved him to a naval hospital near the city where they resided. Although her husband lived almost three months, he never regained consciousness. She told of her daily trips to the hospital, of watching him go from a big man to a mere shadow, and of his apparent agony at times.

We sat in my living room quietly for some time after this part of her story. Then she started to talk again about how a few years later she had met an army officer, fallen in love with him, and married. He came to live in her home and brought with him his three children. Since their marriage, they had experienced much difficulty, in the adjustment of the two families into her home. She had fallen one day going down the outside steps and broken her leg. Her new husband had suffered a heart attack. Now he wanted to buy a home just under construction, feeling they should all begin life in new surroundings. She felt reluctant to give up the home she owned.

After a time I very quietly said to her, "Your first husband didn't just have an accident. He often went out in the night and drove the car. But this time he really did hit the abutment, intending to kill himself in the crash. In addition to the internal injuries, he put his left shoulder out of joint and this caused him considerable pain, since they never did try to set it."

While amazed, she expressed very great relief that, at long last, she could talk to someone who, other than through Spirit, had no way of knowing about the situation. I explained to her that her former husband presently remained earthbound. He came back to their home, especially to the roses in the garden he loved. He resented the intrusion of her new husband and family into a place he had not relinquished by death. This partly caused her continued trouble, particularly since she and her husband had not changed even the bedroom furniture.

It took several counselling sessions and much prayer before this woman began to see that God was really guiding her into a new life. She finally agreed to sell her own house and get rid of the pieces of furniture from her first marriage. When her present husband wished to move some of the rose bushes, she followed the guidance given and asked him not to take any to their new home.

It was exciting to see the change coming in her life as she brought various samples of curtains and rugs to ask advice. Their problems didn't dissolve all at once, but she and her husband gradually began, individually and as a family, to set new goals and change from old to new patterns. They also purchased new furniture instead of moving a piece of the furniture from her first marriage. One of the first rooms completely furnished with everything new was their bedroom. A new sense of family unity developed and in the following years this woman has been a good mother to her second husband's three children.

One very important thing that took place in the realm of the Spirit before any of these events began to occur on the earth plane related to my prayer for her first husband. In this earth life, when a person wants to get something done, it is often a case of knowing the right people to get help. The same is true in the realm of the Spirit. Ever since a little child, I had known people in the Spirit world and had become more knowledgeable through the years.

In the plane where this man's spirit existed, no one could help him. He still suffered much pain, as though conscious of his out-of-joint left shoulder. I prayed for help to come to him, that one of the great servants of Light would break through to where he was and guide him to a higher plane where his needs could be met and his consciousness raised.

I remember the great freedom the day I knew this had really taken place. From that moment on many forces that had been pressing down lifted. I knew my prayers were being answered and that verification would come to my friend on the earth plane. At this time a new freedom came to the family. They made decisions clearly without tensions, and the transition into their new life and home occurred smoothly.

However, this story did not end there. One day as this couple left church, the husband drew me aside and said, "If ever I can do anything for you, I will."

I smiled at him and said, "Yes, you can be the first member of a men's prayer group I have asked the Lord for."

He drew back in shock. "I can do many things, but prayer isn't one of them. You know I never could pray."

I did not let him off. In fact, I told him prayer was the one thing I knew he could do better than all else. He replied, "All these years we have believed you and followed the guidance that came to you for us. If you really believe I am to be your first member, then I will be."

Within a few weeks I sat one Sunday with the seven men for whom I had been praying. Although all members in the same church, they did not know one another in any intimate way. Now they sat in a circle facing one another—an army major, a colonel, men in top business positions and high in government appointments—all beginners in the field of prayer.

From the beginning a wonderful spirit of unity existed between these men because God had selected and chosen them and he always creates unity. True, he had revealed them to me and I had to have the courage to speak and firmly hold to my belief, but I had not chosen any of them.

One very distinguished man got up at our first meeting to say he knew of no reason for his being in such a group. Everything in his life was wonderful, including a beautiful wife, two lovely daughters and a son, plus a good position and financial independence. What did he need with a prayer group?

At this point I exercised my authority as the leader and gave a command to one who was used to giving commands to others. I said quietly, but firmly, "Sit down. You may not know now why God has chosen to put you into such a group as this, but I know that he would not have chosen you without a reason. Whether he reveals that to you today or a year from now I can't say, but I expect you to be faithful and to give your very best to the members of this group." That set the tone and we moved forward.

We learned first of all to remain silent together. Gradually the men began to pray aloud. We took similar prayer assignments for each week, using the same affirmation for the entire week. Each one agreed to spend time in meditation each day. We met for an hour on Sunday mornings at ten o'clock.

The group faced its first test when told we could no longer use the room we had found so conducive to our quiet times. Finally we were given a small cubbyhole into which we could scarcely squeeze, but these executives, with lovely homes and offices, felt that continuity of the group was more important than the place where we met, and they came faithfully each Sunday.

After a year of leadership, I relinquished the role to one of the other members and the group became an all men's group. They also got to move back into the first room. Through the group each member's life has had new beginnings, and they have unleashed great spiritual power individually and collectively. They have learned to pray effectively for others and have accepted the rules of a disciplined prayer life.

Several of the men have known advancement in their professional work. When a change of positions became necessary in a number of their lives, they made them with prayer support, creative interest, and a true sense of divine guidance. In each case the changes proved not only beneficial for the person, but for the whole family.

The man who initially did not know why he had joined such a group faced several crises. When a circulation problem threatened his right leg, he realized for the first time the joy of others effectively praying for him. He received help on necessary medication, guidance about his nutritional diet, and a physical healing that had a profound effect upon him.

When his younger daughter had to undergo surgery for a growth in her arm, and for days the reports created much anxiety and concern for his family, he found the faith that sustained him and helped to bring his whole family through a difficult period.

New dimensions emerged in the members' lives, often to their own amazement and also that of their friends, employers, and working associates. One man, who had always worked for someone else for a nominal salary, decided to break away and to convert the garage of his home to start a business of his own. The men upheld him and his entire venture in prayer. He soon made a success of the new venture and has gained a new sense of his own ability and confidence.

A FLOW OF DIVINE LOVE

In the summer of 1957 our party of eight—three from Germany and five of us from America—boarded a train in Helsinki for our first trip into Russia.

An event that happened in a churchyard in Leningrad became the crowning experience of the trip. One of the members of our group was Bishop Wunderlich of Frankfurt, Germany. We had visited with the priest and others in a large orthodox church and I had stepped outside into the court. There a group of Russian women surrounded me.

They wanted to know simple things. Was I married? Did I have children? How old was I? I couldn't speak Russian but by showing them my ring, holding up fingers and counting off numbers, we established a wonderfull rapport. I looked at the faces of those women, many old beyond their years, other young mothers, and the tears flowed unashamedly down their faces. Then I realized tears streamed from my eyes, too. A great wave of love engulfed us and made us one. They surged forward, each one seeking to touch me, to make the sign of the cross and to say the word "Christian"!

Several months later I attended a lecture at Garrett Theological School in Evanston. Bishop Wunderlich was the guest speaker. He did not know of my presence. As he talked to the student body, he told of his trip into Russia, of the deep inner tensions, bitterness, resentments, and hate it stirred up within him. He said those feelings became more intense as we daily traveled and mingled with the Russian people who had caused so much suffering among the Germans in the Second World War and following. He could feel no Christian love, no forgiveness within him toward those people.

"Then one day," he said, "I watched as a simple little woman from America won the hearts of a group of Russian women. As I stood in the shadow of the building, hidden from everyone, I witnessed an event that melted the frozen mass within me and I was caught up in the flow of a divine love that set me free. She was able to communicate with them in a marvelous way, wept tears with them, permitted them to touch her and love her as the Christ in their midst. The miracle happened in my life when I, too, became lost to myself in the flow of love between these people. I wondered if it would last. It has and it has increased within me, giving me new freedom, life, and energy."

As he was greeting the students later he caught sight of me on the edge of the crowd. Exclaiming with great delight, "She is here," he rushed toward me to greet me and to take me into the circle with him.

WASHING OF FEET
AND A HEALTH CRISIS

An anxious husband contacted me one day to ask whether or not I would see his wife. I hesitated because I knew she had many complex problems, and I did not feel capable of ministering to them. However, when he told me he had just returned from a trip to Johns Hopkins where her doctor had found a lump in her breast, and this had thrown her into a very great frenzy, I consented to see her.

I realized soon after she came into my home that this woman was near hysteria. I wasn't at all sure I could handle, or should handle, the situation. I let her talk for some time and quietly listened to her, but I knew this wasn't the answer. So after a time I asked her if she would permit me to do something for her, to let me wash her feet.

At first she expressed great surprise that I would want to do something like that for her, but the day was hot, so she slipped off her shoes and said, "Alice, if you will wash my feet, I will be happy to let you." I got a basin of warm water, and with a clean towel and cloth I bent down and began to wash her feet.

All the time I talked to her quietly in a very soothing voice, and as I rubbed her feet and moved my hands across them and underneath them, touching certain nerve ends and gently massaging them, she began to relax. I could almost feel the tension going out of her body, and her whole being became almost one of ease. Then I very carefully dried her feet on the towel and covered them up while I went and got some of my precious bath oil perfume, which turned out to be her favorite. She was overwhelmed that I would use it to rub onto the flesh and muscles of her feet.

It seemed as though, in the ministry of the washing of her feet and the rubbing of the oil into her flesh, we became as one, servant and the served, and love flowed in a very real way between us. She left in a tranquil frame of mind, and at least I felt that I had done all that I could for her.

The next day she went again to Johns Hopkins to make arrangements to have the lump removed from her breast. Her doctor on examination could not locate the lump. It had disappeared. He called in other specialists, and they too did an examination, but no one could find any sign of a lump in her breast. She came home rejoicing that the one thing she feared had been taken from her, and she did not have to go through immediate surgery.

Her doctor was rather upset by the whole happening and could not understand how something could be there one day and not the next. He phoned me from Baltimore to ask me what I had done when his patient visited me. Very simply, but very quietly, I told him of her state of nerves when she came to my home, and of how I ministered to her by the washing of her feet. I explained that at no time had I touched her breast or in any way tried to minister to that part of her body. Nor had I discussed with her the many other problems she had. I rejoiced that the cause of her fear had been lifted from her.

WASHING OF FEET
AND SPIRITUAL RELEASE

The woman who sat in our library, had come for prayer help several times in relation to her family. But now she talked about herself. As I listened. my attention focused on her feet, so much so that after awhile I asked her to join me in a time of silence as I wished to receive guidance about this strong pull toward her feet.

When we had finished the silence I asked her if she would permit me to wash her feet. Visibly shocked, she replied, "I let no one see my feet." I asked why. "Because they are ugly," she replied. I asked her why she felt this way, and she told me that when she was about five or six, she had a skin disease on her feet.

Apparently the lady who cared for her kept telling her about her ugly feet. Eventually they healed but the picture of "ugly feet" remained fastened in her mind. We sat in the silence for sometime and then she said, "But if you will wash my feet I will let you." While I got a basin of water and a towel she slipped off her shoes and stockings.

She put her foot into the basin and I began to wash and to pray for the healing that I knew must come to set this woman free. Perfectly formed, beautiful in color and softness of skin, her feet had no corns or callouses. I washed them and rubbed them with sweet smelling oil. Then together we looked at them. For the first time in many years she listened as someone told her that her feet were beautiful, prayed for the healing of her thoughts about them, thanked God for them, and dedicated them to him.

This event began the release of this person, not only about her feet but in other areas of her life where she found that the thought forms created early in her life were causing blocks and conflicts. She began to follow a discipline of study and prayer under good teaching and guidance, and later came into a meditation group that was meaningful to her and permeated the lives of her family.

SPEAKING IN TONGUES

Glossolalia, or speaking in or with tongues, has become a controversial subject in these past few years as it manifests itself in various ways, places, and groups. Most people in Christian circles today know something about the subject, but relatively few have experienced it as a healing force rather than a force that often splinters a personality.

I knew nothing about this phenomenon except for having studied the biblical accounts in Acts 2 and in 1 Corinthians 14 when I went with my husband as the only American woman delegate to the first Lay Academy held in Bad Ball, Germany, following World War II in the summer of 1951. I saw evidence of war everywhere, and this brought very real memories as I had had brothers serve in the Canadian Navy and Air Force.

One of the high moments of the conference was the singing of hymns before the lectures. Each one sang in his own language, which became a mighty chorus of voices. One evening as we finished one of the great hymns of the church, the gentleman standing next to me (he had known my husband several years in the ecumenical work) turned to me in amazement with the statement, "Why don't you speak to me in German, Mrs. Ward?" Astonished, I explained that I did not know a word of the German language. "But," he continued, "you most certainly do. You sang that entire hymn in the most beautiful voice and in perfect German! It was so wonderful that I did not sing a note myself, but just stood and listened to you."

That shocked me because, although I love music, I do not know how to sing and have no voice for it.

The same thing happened on another occasion during the same conference when I was standing next to a lady from Holland. She, too, heard the entire hymn sung in her own language and in a perfectly beautiful voice. Nothing I could say seemed to convince those people otherwise. They had both heard and received a wonderful blessing and in a language they knew. I felt bewildered and in need of an explanation. In both cases, I had been completely caught up in the Spirit, conscious only of the great thrill of his presence.

Years later when the man visited our home on Long Island

he recalled the experience and verified the great blessing in his life at a time when the song had gone out of his heart through the war years. Then as he heard the great hymn sung once again, something had come alive within him and a new song was born. I met the Dutch lady later also and she gave a similar witness. She had come to the conference having lost every living relative and had chosen to go and serve a church just inside the eastern zone of Berlin. For her, too, it became a new song of hope and faith.

SPIRITUAL CONTROL BY THE MASTER

Asked to participate in an all day ministers' seminar in which my responsibility was to lead discussion on the topic of confronting sickness and crisis in one's personal life, in the family and the larger community, I carefully prepared my lecture, on both content and length. My assignment was to lead three groups before the noon break.

The first one went as planned and the material seemed well received. As the second group came in, I was surprised to see one particular lady sitting on the front row. At the same time, I felt a change coming over me, as though another person was taking control.

When I began to speak, I was amazed at what I heard. I was giving a lecture on the correct topic, but in an entirely new voice and format. I was not speaking; another person was speaking through me, using correctly the prepared material. When the lecture ended, many persons came up to thank me and especially the minister sitting next to the lady, who, it turned out, was his wife. He had taken the liberty to bring her and was deeply grateful for what I said.

Still partially dazed when the third group filed in, I felt relieved to see all men facing me. The lecture and entire period went as planned, as smoothly as the first one. My mind still asked the question, "Why?" Then I found myself seated next to the lady and her husband at lunch. She began telling me about herself.

She had ceased feeling like a person and considered herself nothing but a living case history for a group of doctors. A radical mastectomy had caused this complete rejection of herself. One could sense the inner tensions that existed, also those between herself and her minister-husband. I inquired about what had made her feel this way. She told me that added to the surgery itself had been the exposure to almost constant examination by a group of doctors and medical students. She lived in dread of those examinations and couldn't speak about it. This had resulted in a repulsion against herself.

Quietly, I began to tell her of the fact that I, too, had had similar surgery. I noted that only once had a team of doctors surprised me in such a way, but I had requested protection against such exposure. I explained how I had begun to rehabilitate myself and of the things my husband and I had done in our marriage and family to meet the change successfully. Her husband, I knew, had been greatly helped during the lecture and he seemed to take on a new attitude as I shared experiences with them.

At that time I knew the amazing love and wisdom of an ever present God. Had I given the lecture as I had planned, unknowingly, it could have hurt this woman. But the Spirit took control and she and others realized a great healing blessing.

IV
POWER OF PRAYER AND SILENCE

INTRODUCTION

The culmination in many ways of Alice's search for new life in the Spirit came with her developing capacity to engage in effective prayer and sustained silence. The illustrations in this chapter are only a few of the almost countless experiences she had in her private prayer life and its effect on the lives of others.

About twelve years before her death, we faced together fundamental questions involving our individual growth spiritually and the values of our marriage. We came to the conclusion after much prayer, thought, and discussion that we were ready to gamble individually and as a couple on the possibility of becoming genuinely autonomous as persons, and at the same time interdependent as a couple.

I had begun to recognize her capacities as a sensitive being with unusual qualities of insight into persons and events, intuitive powers, and gifts of healing. I knew these needed expression and the freedom to grow. We realized that the result might disrupt our marriage, but we believed sincerely that it was all worth the gamble. In the long run, we both became new persons. Her life flowered into the pristine, majestic qualities which touched the lives of so many and brought God so close. I began slowly to respond to new dimensions of spiritual meanings and possibilities.

For both of us prayer became the center of these new dimensions. For the first time we realized that prayer was not simply liturgy, or cries of desperation, or attempts to influence the Deity to give or do things. It became a means of direct encounter with God and the most effective channel for experiencing a surge of spiritual power. It, in short, became the experience of God himself.

When this realization emerged, many things fell into place. Our theological questions were cared for basically. We no longer had any question about the reality of God. We found it easy to believe in miracles. Nothing became impossible and we had no need to put limitation on any experience of the spirit or body. This was the source of a quality of freedom which transcended anything we had ever known. Our life together became an exciting new adventure which continued with growing intensity until her death, despite her great suffering with cancer. Truly, the find of the ages for us was prayer, reflective meditation, and deep silence.   —A. D. W.

A CHILD IS BORN

In answer to a frantic telephone call one day I became involved in the birth of a child. A minister friend called to ask for prayer for a young woman who had been for several hours in the delivery room. He was sitting with the young husband, a native of another country, as he waited for his wife to deliver their first child. Both of the couple were working on their education in this country when they discovered that the wife was pregnant. This caused them some difficulty in deciding how they would arrange their financial situation in the months ahead.

They kept pushing the impending event further and further from them. When the birth pains suddenly struck the girl, she was not prepared for them, believing that the baby was not due for several weeks. The doctor had come down to inform the husband and to ask whether or not he could in any way help his wife because it seemed as though she refused to permit the birth of the baby. She kept pulling it back up into her body so that the doctor could not bring about the birth naturally. He feared both for her life and for the life of the child.

At this point I received the telephone call for prayer. I asked the minister to take the young husband down into the chapel of the hospital and there to kneel at the altar and relinquish this woman to Christ. Then they should envision this new child coming into the world as a free soul completely released from the mother's physical body and beginning his new life on this earth with joy and with a burst of happiness as he emerged from her body.

I entered into the silence and asked for the help of one of the saints whom I have come to know and who ministers to little children. She readily appeared before me and said she would assist in the birth of this child and suggested that there was no further cause for anxiety. Within an hour I had a phone call from the minister saying that a beautiful baby boy had been born and the doctor had come to tell them that it seemed as though it all happened in a wonderful way with great ease. The baby was normal and in fine condition, and so was the mother. I have seen this child on occasion since, and he is a very radiant, happy soul and has brought great blessing to both of his parents.

PRAYER LIFE

One of the very promising young women in my Sunday afternoon prayer group had made great strides in her prayer discipline. But I knew she had difficulty in her nutritional discipline. Although many persons had offered much prayer for her, I felt that unless some new insights came to her as to what she was doing to herself, eventually much of the prayer discipline would break down too.

In the course of our work we decided to have a series of lectures on nutrition with a fine doctor in charge. I tried to convince her that this was her real opportunity to come and to receive the information she needed. But she said she had quite a few other commitments and would not be able to do it at this time. Disappointed because I felt in having these lectures I would be able to lift my prayer burden for her and in some way get her to read or relate herself to the real cause of her problem, I did not know how to persuade her to come.

However, when the lecture series was completely paid for and subscribed to, I called her one day and said, "Are you free on Wednesday night? Will you come to one lecture? I really do believe that you should hear what this man has to say tonight." She agreed, and I said, "It won't cost you anything because the course is completely paid for and you can be my guest."

She came and that evening the medical doctor spoke on hypoglycemia (an abnormal disease of sugar in the blood) and its effect. He pointed out that people could have it for many years, not know what was wrong with them, and be doctoring for many other things. Right away this sounded familiar to her. She knew that she should have a test made. She also realized that she had long sidestepped this discipline because it meant restriction on certain things she had enjoyed both privately and socially.

The next day she went and had the tests made. They indicated she had a severe case of hypoglycemia. A dedicated person and an intelligent person, she immediately set herself on a new course and followed with precision the diet and other treatments necessary to restore her physical body in balance again.

After almost a year a remarkable change occurred. Her prayer life had lost the sense of futility, and the feeling that God was not hearing and answering her prayers. Nor did she feel that somehow some miracle would occur outside herself that would cause a change. She realized that she was responsible for much of the change taking place in her life and that such change requires a daily discipline.

The young woman moved forward into a whole new life, not only of the spirit, but of the body and of the mind. I rejoiced to see that wholeness can come, but only when all parts are working together in harmony. God does help those who help themselves, and he will not intervene in those things which we can do ourselves. When one realizes we are all workers together with God, all things become possible.

NEW LIFE FOR A YOUNG ADULT

A young woman asked one day if I would see her. She had gone to so many psychiatrists and had wearied of telling the same story and getting the same answers. She felt that she had reached her limit. Then someone suggested that perhaps I would talk to her.

One evening she came out to my home. As we sat together, I asked her if she would be willing to sit in the silence for sometime before she began to tell me her story so that perhaps I would learn much of it without having her repeat it.

For sometime we sat in the silence. As we communed with God, a lovely lady appeared beside her. I knew it was her mother because of the resemblance. A middle-aged man also appeared and stood apart from her, though still in the orbit of her consciousness and life. The mother revealed to me that this child was born out of wedlock, and that she had given the years of her life for the girl. She had worked to assure her education and her fine development as a lady.

The mother had died as a young woman. Obviously this girl suffered from the knowledge that she was an illegitimate child and that she did not have the family contact enjoyed by so many other people, especially her friends. She needed the confidence, help, and love of parents.

When we finished our time of quietness and prayer, I told her about the person who had appeared in the room while we were in prayer. She said, "That is my mother, but my mother is dead." Then I explained the life of the spirit and of how her mother, very concerned about her, had brought her to me.

I tactfully told her that I knew something, too, about her struggles in life and that she did not have to tell me about all the things that had happened and of the difficulties she had had or the things that she had tried to overcome. I knew no matter how much education or how beautifully she dressed, she could not erase from her mind the fact that she had not had a normal childhood, but had been raised in a children's home.

She was amazed that she did not have to tell all her story and that it had come through the love of her mother in a beautiful way. I only mentioned the middle-aged man who had appeared since her mother had been very careful not to divulge anything about him. I also pointed out to her that one reason why she had been guided to me was the deep concern of her mother that her daughter would not make or be lured into making the same mistake her mother had made. Her mother seemed to know that the possibility of making this mistake was very present at this particular time. The daughter would have to take definite action and make certain decisions if she were to save herself from making the same mistake that her mother had made years before.

During the next week, I had a telephone call from her telling me she had broken off with the middle-aged man that I had seen the night she visited my home. This would be quite difficult for her because she had become, over a period of time, quite involved in this situation. I was firm with her. If she expected help and counseling in this matter, she also had to make very definite decisions, stick by them, and start to reorient her life. She was so anxious for help that she agreed to do what I advised as far as disciplines.

I first advised her to come to the evening teaching class of our healing service, quite a new venture for her. She would rather have come into my prayer group immediately and been under my surveillance, but I could not permit this. She had to go into my husband's teaching class and complete two full courses before she could come into any prayer group.

The one request I made of her was that if she started into this work, she must be faithful each Sunday or else tell me why she couldn't be there. I could not allow any freedom to slip back into the same mode of living she had had before. She came to the classes and to the healing service that followed, and except for a few times when she has been away or had an engagement, she attended regularly all the classes and services. Then she moved up into the prayer groups and showed real progress.

This was not only a discipline for her on Sunday, but a daily discipline in her life as well. She sought and obtained the true guidance at a particular time in her life. She has followed these disciplines; she has turned from a life that would have brought unhappiness and repeated former things from which she could not seem to release herself, to a life developing rich and full.

She has met new people, found new interests, and has become a fine and respected young lady both in the church, with her friends and in her social circle. Gradually, she has come to believe that people do love her and that the world does contain love for her, that she is a true child of God, and that she has nothing of which to be ashamed. As she has come to believe this, she has also realized that she now has love within her to give to others. This has been a new experience for this lonely person.

THE MUSIC OF THE SPHERES

In the formation of our Ministry of Prayer and Health at

Foundry United Methodist Church, Washington, D. C., the pastor's wife had shared with us in the form and structure of the work. Months after the pastor began his ministry at Foundry he told us at one of our meetings that his wife was going into the hospital for surgery. It was around the middle of February and he asked us to pray especially for her.

On the morning of her surgery I went into the library, also our Prayer room, to be in silence during the period of the operation. Sometimes, during periods such as this, I am directed by the Spirit to sit down on the floor or to lie on the floor completely relaxed. This morning I was instructed to lie flat on the floor and give myself entirely to the use of the Spirit during this time of another person's surgery.

As I entered into the silence, I felt that my whole body was completely relaxed, lifted and transmuted into a realm of spiritual awareness. I felt that the surgery taking place in the hospital here in Washington was also moving in an identical relaxed fashion, that the Spirit of our pastor's wife was lifted above her physical body, and peace and joy were present in the operating room. After receiving this stillness and awareness, I became aware of joy and freedom surging through my entire being. Then I heard music and listened as the music came closer to me and increased in its beauty. Gradually this music, sung by a heavenly choir, enveloped me. The words came very clearly: "Now, thank we all our God with heart and hands and voices, who wondrous things hath done; In whom his world rejoices; Who from our mother's arms, hath blessed us on our way with countless gifts of love, and still is ours today."

I heard three entire stanzas of this hymn. When it ended, it seemed as though other great choirs of Heaven joined in this majestic hymn of praise. They, too, sang it over and over again until I did not want to break free from the enveloping atonement with the person being prayed for in the Spirit. I knew that all was well with our pastor's wife, and felt great rejoicing, not only by her doctors, but also within herself and her family.

In a short while the telephone rang. Her husband told me that the operation had ended, that the doctors were happy with the way it turned out, that his wife was fine, that he was so thankful for prayer. Then I shared with him my wonderful experience during the time of the surgery, that I, too had had the most glorious experience I had ever known, and that all Heaven shared with him in his relief and the joy of his wife in the success of her operation.

This wonderful joy stayed with me. I would sit in the silence each day during our pastor's wife's recovery and, coming into contemplation, mention her name to the Lord. Then the music would encompass and envelop us. I felt transported into another realm by this wonderful music. I am sure in some mysterious way this established a field of grace within me because within the next few days, while the pastor's wife remained in the hospital, we faced a crisis with our son, John, who required brain surgery following an accident.

The pastor was in the hospital visiting his wife the day John was rushed into emergency when neither Dudley nor I could be present. The pastor established a wonderful relationship with John immediately. This anthem just seemed to carry over into our mutual experience—the pastor's wife's and John's recovery.

Such a spiritual experience, in relationship to any person whom one does not know very well in a physical way, can become a transforming experience. Each time I saw this woman, or heard her sing in the choir, or my thoughts went to her, I thought of her in connection with music. I especially thought of the marvelous experience I had had in prayer for her in relationship to the music from other than this world. It was very much part of her life and had now become very much a part of my life through my prayers for her.

In the spring of 1965 one of the morning worship services at Foundry Church centered on appreciation of music. Following the service the congregation was asked to come to the altar rail of the church and thank the choir members for the music that they had provided. I went forward and when I shook the hand of the pastor's wife, she said, "I have been meaning to call you. I am leaving today to go out to see my father. He's going to have surgery tomorrow and I want to be there." I asked her his name and she gave it to me. I told her I would pray for him.

Later it occurred to me that I should know approximately

what time the surgery would take place and I called to find out. The pastor's wife said, "It will be at nine o'clock their time, eight o'clock our time." This suited my time of prayer very well because the children and Dudley had left the house and I was able to go once again into the library early in the morning, and give myself completely for the use of the Spirit during the surgery of her father.

A sense of being attuned and at one with the Spirit came very quickly that morning, and I felt that the mere mention of this man's name put me into a wonderful relationship with God. I moved into this period of contemplation so that I could be used as a vehicle through which strength and blessing could come to him during his surgery. In the silence I soon became aware of music. It seemed at a distance.

For awhile I could not discern the words or tune, but I knew it was a wonderful hymn and anthem. It did not come clearly for quite some time and then it moved closer and enveloped me.

I heard the hosts of Heaven; it seemed all the choirs of Heaven, especially great male voices, wonderfully strong, were singing. The great victory and praise in the hymn lifted me to the Heavens. I felt my whole being transported into the presence of the Most High. I knew I was not just being used but the power of the blessing coming to me was of transcendent nature.

The music rose to a great swell of praise and alleluia. As I prayed for this man's health and healing, I could feel healing moving through my entire being also. It was not a motion in one direction, but a full orbit or circle, gathering all within it, and this music was part of the great encompassing light that brought us into its full orbit. The pastor's wife was part of this, of the circle, of the whole we were experiencing. I could not hear this great music in English. It came with full swells but in a foreign tongue.

After my period of silence and contemplation ended and I knew I had to begin my household tasks, this great music stayed with me. I thought again and again, "I'll go sit down in the silence and surely I will hear it and know it, word for word because I have heard it sung, and I have sung it myself." It was rather tantalizing. I found I was very often just sitting quietly, saying, "Lord, reveal it to me. Let me hear it in my own language." But it did not come that way. It always came in the foreign language.

Often when I went to bed at night, this music would drift in and I would think in the morning I will know it in English, and not have to wonder what it is any more. Again and again the great music would come to me in the silence of my prayer period, yet always in the same language.

Speaking to our pastor about his wife's father and inquiring about his surgery, I told him of the experience and of the wonderful music. I mentioned that I did not know the name of this hymn and anthem in English. I knew the anthem and I knew I had heard it sung, but I did not know the words in English. As the days went by, the Spirit told me that I should not seek to know this in English. This hymn had been sung in the father's native tongue. That was the way the Heavenly Hosts would sing it for him. In my prayers for him I had to realize that the Spirit world would relate to him in his natural and native tongue.

In time the Spirit would make known to me if I was patient and released it completely as a great blessing to the family—in his own time and in the place he chose. I was no longer to inquire or seek it for myself. In talking with our pastor's wife upon her return, I told her this. I said I did not know the language used but I thought it might be German. I asked her whether or not her father was of German descent, and she said he was. She also said he had a fine voice, sang in the choir when younger, and was a lover of music.

I rested in this, thankful that I had had a share in this ministry, feeling I was being used in his recovery. Often when in communion with the Spirit for my own refreshment, this man's name would come into my consciousness, and upon releasing the name to the Spirit, I would be enveloped in this music. I felt so wonderfully refreshed and reenergized and my spirits lifted as I heard this great anthem sung again in a tongue I neither spoke nor read.

Never at any time did I try to draw the music to myself. Never did I again seek to know it or have it translated by

Spirit. I entered into the joy of the swelling praises and received the blessing given in it through Spirit and through the tongue in which it was sung. I thanked God for the opportunity to pray for such a great soul. The mere coming into silent communion with God, bringing this man or the mention of his name, immediately transported me into this realm of music and praise.

On Sunday, July 31, 1966 I went to the 9:30 A.M. service at Foundry Church. I expected Dudley in from London so it was already a special day in our lives. A guest speaker preached on the sermon topic, "The Search for Self." These three weeks in which Dudley had been away were fruitful days for him and for us who stayed at home. I was in a very relaxed, happy, receptive mood this morning.

The choir began to sing the offertory anthem, the title "Sauda Anima" not meaning anything in particular to me. But once they began to sing, I heard again the Heavenly Hosts and I knew this was the anthem! This was it! Present in the church, vibrating in every current, the music rang like a mighty choir within me. I was wholly involved—body, mind, and soul. I quickly wrote down on the side of my bulletin the words:

> Father like he tends and spares us
> In his hands he gently bears us
> Saints triumphant bow before Him
> Gathered in from every race.
> Hallelujah.
> Praise with us, the God of grace.

I knew I had heard the great anthem. It was exulting, thrilling, beyond words. I stopped one of the soloists after the service and asked her where I could get a copy of the anthem, and she said, "My dear, I'll give you mine; we can spare one." I came home and looked through our books on hymns. I read again the history of the hymn I had heard when the pastor's wife went through surgery—"Now Thank We All Our God," No. 7 in the old Methodist Hymn Book.

This hymn was written by Rinkert about 1636 in Germany.

First sung in Leipzig, Germany on June 25, 1840 at a celebration to honor the invention of printing, it had been chosen as the great hymn of thanksgiving. Katherine Winkworth had translated it into English in the 1850's.

I looked up the anthem, also in our hymn book, (No. 77) "Praise My Soul, the King of Heaven." This hymn was written by Henry Lyte, an Englishman and minister of the Church of England, around 1834 (although I heard it sung in German for the benefit of the one for whom I prayed). It was the happiest of all his versions of the Psalms. He also authored "Abide With Me." His great religious transforming experience came while ministering to a neighboring clergyman, with whom he had spent considerable time prior to the friend's death. In writing about this experience, he said: "I was greatly affected by the whole matter and brought to look at life and its issues with a different eye than before. I began to study my Bible and preach in another manner than I had previously done." During this period he wrote the great hymn "Praise My Soul, the King of Heaven."

Contemplating these events, I realized that through the wonderful love of God expressed in music, the hymn that came for the pastor's wife in my time of silence for her would come in her own native tongue, English. In the prayer for her father, the hymn for him would also come in his native tongue, German.

This is the one Universal Mind—God. This all encompassing love was expressed to me, in the fullness of time, as I sat in church that July Sunday and listened to our own choir singing the anthem. I was in the right place, at the right time, to receive the fulfillment of the promise that I would one day hear the words of the great anthem in my native tongue, English. These experiences made meaningful the years in which I have daily sought and willingly accepted the discipline and obedience to what it means to become thoroughly involved in prayer. I believe that both our pastor's wife and her father are great souls. One I have met and know slightly; the other I have never met. Yet I know that in the Spirit they are known by other great spiritual persons and powers. They are known for their praise and thanksgiving and the choirs of Heaven sing at the mention of their names.

No man is an island and I, in a wonderful but strange and mysterious way, have been part of two beautiful spirits. I pray in the world to come I will continue to be a part of their unfolding and enlightenment and their wonderful relationship to music. Although I play no instrument or sing, through contemplative meditation I am attuned to the "music of the spheres."

The Spirit revealed to me that the art of prayer is the highest art in the world. Coming into an awareness of this art all other arts are open to one's understanding, enjoyment, and appreciation.

A PRAYER MEDITATION FOR A PASTOR

This meditation came to me in my quiet time on September 9, 1966 at 9 A.M. when the pastor of Foundry United Methodist Church was facing immediate surgery:

The voices all will be stilled and you will hear the inner voice of the true God. Of yourself you could not do this. It was impossible for you to shut out the many voices around you seeking to attract your attention, offering you such enticements, holding up mirrors that caused a refraction of the light. Many things appear double to you and you are unable to draw them into a true focus.

In the period of surgery and anesthesia, all these forces will fall from you. The single eye of the Spirit will be opened and your spirit will discern it. You will be given a new life—a personality that will have love and dominion over the forces clammering for your attention. You will hear the one true Voice and understand his command for your life. Even now he speaks to you. You are encompassed about with a host of angels. No negative forces can get through. It is amazing the authority and order they have. The doctors, nurses, attendants do not realize it but they are all under command. They are doing things as the Spirit directs. Your physical body is wonderfully relaxed. The mechanical work will be accomplished speedily. All is well!

You are not to be fooled by this physical well-being that will manifest itself in a short period of time. You are to take this time, a week or so longer than even the doctor may think necessary, to assimilate this new dimension that now is yours in the Spirit. You will not comprehend it all at once. It may appear differently from time to time. You can perceive its true meaning only in silence. Guard this very carefully. Your whole future depends on this. Let no man take this from you.

All the voices will be stilled this morning. This was the one thing you said to me the day I gave you the cross to carry with you around the world—that you wanted to "just get away from the many voices." One can never do that while in earth consciousness. This is what I was trying to say about the Cross as symbol. Only in the victory that was achieved on the Cross can one be lifted to a consciousness that transcends the clamour of many voices. Once you hear the Voice you will forever be free from the din of chatter.

> Oh what a glorious morning
> When the stars begin to shine!

You will now be able truly to see your wife, in the Spirit, the true person. The old image with its limitations and fears will disappear. She will emerge as a person in light. You will find you at-one-ment—your vocation together, the true mission for your life. She has within her all that is required to complement you. This will not emerge all at once for either of you. Gradually as you begin to perceive this, you will see the picture change. It will be one perfectly complementing the other. This will create a strength that will in time flow to many lives. In this unity you will both grow strong as persons and not be diminished by outside forces. This will be true expansion for all within each one of you. Alone neither one of you could have realized this.

Your colors—your Spirit colors—complement one another perfectly. This was present the night you were married at the high altar of the church. Your ministry to Foundry Church was sealed in your vows. This is your true mission, the star in the sky you saw together that night. This is the gift that was born or consummated that night.

It was the uniting of the perfect parts to compose the Light that in the fullness of time would come to Foundry and to the altar of this church. Alone you are incomplete. Together the light goes on.

The power flows. Two people do become one in color because they mix to make one color. This is the morning! The Star begins to shine in all its dazzling radiance, now visible against the morning sky, not just against the darkness of the night. Rather it appears in full light, dazzling. Today each of you has discovered your mixing color and what a wonderful discovery to know that it has been perfect all the time.

> Oh what a beautiful morning
> When the stars begin to shine
> I will give you the bright light
> and His morning star.

It is as though this morning you were married in the Spirit. You became *one* in Spirit. This marriage took place in the morning at the high altar of Foundry Church and when you turned to face the church it was filled with people from every land. They saw a great light as you joined hands and turned to face them.

The radiance was dazzling and the rays went out on all sides. The people moved toward the light and souls surrounded you, yet you stood together free. There was a free circulation around you. The light radiated with rays in a beautiful color from you both. You did nothing; the Light did all! All the people sang:

> Love divine, all loves excelling
> Joy of heaven to earth come down.
> Fix in us thy humble dwelling,
> All thy faithful mercies crown.

I completed the meditation at 10:45. The hymn I heard the congregation or the multitude of souls assembled in the church sing for our pastor and his wife, as they turned from the altar is No. 372 in *The Methodist Hymnal*. I was glad to know the number seven was in the center. I knew nothing about their wedding except that they told our daughter, Dianne, they were married at Foundry on Christmas Eve, I believe.

This meditation followed early morning prayer by Dudley and me in the library at home. Our pastor and his wife were especially central in these prayers. After I concluded the meditation, these events occurred:

Dudley came home about 10:55 to take our son, John, to Alexandria for registration at St. Stephen's School. John was still looking at television so he had to get washed and dressed. Dudley was here when the pastor's wife called shortly after eleven and we had prayer together for the second time. Then Dudley left at 11:20 for the school.

In the stillness of the library I continued to lie on the floor. Complete peace, relaxation, came over me, and I became conscious of being lifted by spiritual forces. An operating room came into focus, a room filled with supreme calmness, precision and confidence.

The prayer power seemed to provide a plank on which our pastor's spiritual body rested. Relaxed and interested, he turned so he could see all that was happening to the physical body on the operating table.

Then, quite unexpectedly, I felt a sudden jab in my back, as though a long needle entered my spine, and I almost cried out from the intense pain. Slowly a numbness spread out from this center downward over the abdomen, and all feeling left me. The operation proceeded very calmly. The surgeon removed the obstructions like seeds; they did not break. Very pleased, the surgeon completed the necessary procedures speedily. Then the pastor's spirit body reentered the physical. It spread to every atom with perfect circulation, and there was receptivity and joy in the completeness of the whole person.

The spiritual persons who came to assist in the time of surgery each gave a blessing to the pastor before they withdrew. It was a beautiful thing to witness. God had used these few moments in time to accomplish many great and wonderful things in the life of our dynamic minister.

This meditation ended at 12:15. I felt in my prayers like a small child standing on tiptoe waiting for some wonderful thing to happen, like a child feels on Christmas Eve.

A SPIRITUAL VISION AND A HEALING

We had known a certain ministerial colleague over a number of years, and had become close friends with him and his wife. However, we never had met or known any of his paternal family or their history. At various times of decision and need our friend had asked for my prayers.

During one of my prayer periods, on a Saturday morning, I was not concentrating on him, but I saw a vision of three men—a father in the center with a son on each side. I noted a strong family resemblance and could distinguish the one person as our friend. It became clear the older persons were his father, who had died several years before, and a brother. I sensed a real pathos in the situation. Our friend's brother needed a brother's help and the father, in the true paternal role, anxiously sought to bring them together.

The events began to unfold over the next hours. I evidenced the great concern of the father to get a message through to his son. The other son was traveling from his home to a place near where his brother lived. However, the father did not feel free to approach him to help in his present trouble.

I lived through this unfolding drama in the morning, afternoon, and into the evening. I felt at times the pressure to phone our friend, but hesitated as all my knowledge came from the Spirit, and I had no other confirmation. Finally, I released it all to the Spirit and knew that if I had a role to play, I would have to act soon in the right way and time. I said, "If this be of God, I stand willing to serve to be part of a healing, but let me know before this day is done."

I knew that our friend was leaving on an extensive trip to distant countries the next morning. Around 11:30 the same day I was ironing my son's pants for Sunday School the next day. The phone rang and I heard our friend say, "I am sitting at my desk and everything I know is in order. I am ready for the trip and yet even at this late hour, I felt compelled to phone you. What is it about?"

I told him of my day, of the progressive vision of his father and brother, and also of the events that I knew had taken place that day in his vicinity. He was amazed at my knowledge of his brother's name and his difficulties. He had heard something about the trouble, but did not know the concern at this time. I told him that his brother had been in the city very close to where he lived that day and was probably now on his way home.

Our friend phoned immediately to where his brother lived down state. The babysitter said that he would call her about midway on his return trip home. Our friend left a message for his brother to call, which he did before midnight from a phone booth on the highway.

This began a series of events that eventually brought about the healing of relationships between the two brothers and their families.

This new relationship within the family circle broadened his work relationships and attitudes. As he had discovered the soul within his own brother, he was confronted with the soul within his fellowmen and more particularly, his own son. This was a new experience for one who, by worldly standards had arrived. However, for the first time he would face a personal attack—a threat to his security, position, and success. Whenever he asked me for spiritual help, it came clearly and incisively that he would receive assistance so he would be able to stand under fire, to learn what honesty meant for him.

During this time, another vision concerning our friend appeared. I had no way of knowing where he had lived as a youth, nor what his father's occupation was. One day when our friend phoned, asking for prayer help, his father appeared in a railway man's suit with a cap on his head, standing outside a railroad station near the tracks. He had in his right hand a lighted lantern that kept swinging and was quietly standing watch.

I described what I had seen to our friend, and he, hundreds of miles away from me, said, "That is the true picture of my father.

He was a railroad man all his life, the watchman for the train in our hometown."

I replied, "Yes, he had just a humble job on this earth, but he was a great man of God and he says to you, 'Stand there and swing the light.'"

During more times of crisis, this man stood firm and kept swinging the light. This encounter brought about a deep healing, a true conviction of the communion of saints, the reality of eternal life, and the presence of the Holy Spirit in his life.

V
HEALING AND HEALTH

INTRODUCTION

The concern for physical health and well-being is as old and universal as human beings. In these later times an almost equal concern for psychological and mental health has emerged. However, for those who live in the Judeo-Christian tradition, a more comprehensive concern for the whole person has grown to be an essential part of that faith.

In many ways this culminated in the teaching and work of Jesus, but did not stop there, for it has become central to the life and work of the Christian church. The church has become increasingly aware that the term "wholeness"—physical, psychological, social, and spiritual well-being—most adequately expresses the intention of God for his people. The church has not always placed crucial emphasis on this side of its life, but a genuine revival of this message has occurred in recent years.

For Alice this was a natural development of her growth in prayer and was given a personal urgency through the long struggle with cancer.* Her capacities as a healer became increasingly evident. Her insights into the spiritual and psychological difficulties, needs and possibilities of persons became widely known, and literally hundreds of people visited her.

As her ministry increased, it became apparent that new concepts were natural additions. For example, "openness" is a fundamental necessity to those seeking healing—openness to the idea that God can heal, to the movement of the Holy Spirit, to the essential therapies of medical and psychological sciences, to the supporting influence of a company of faithful intercessors. Another word is "light," symbolizing the presence and beauty of the power of God as it moves into and through one's being. An

---

* The full story is told in *I Remain Unvanquished,* published by Abingdon Press in 1970.

essential concept is that of "movement." Humans hold a common assumption that development and health only occur in struggle, leading to eventual control, even domination, over self and environment and substantial influence on other persons. While this assumption has considerable truth, and much of this book will testify to its validity, it is not by any means the entire story.

We can learn a great deal in the art of submission of self to influences and directions that bring often radically different perspectives and possibilities into one's life. It is difficult, especially for western minds, to comprehend this. However, our Judeo-Christian tradition is replete with teachings and events which attest to its validity.

The biblical record is very largely the discovery of a new personal and corporate awareness of growth potential and realization by those who followed, and submitted willingly to, the work of God in human life. "Make me a captive, Lord, then I shall be truly free," is probably the most succinct way of saying it.

The incidents in this book, this chapter in particular, are included to point in the direction of that frame of mind, of spirit, and of action, conducive to both a necessary submission to the Holy Spirit and the ability to exert one's own capacities.

The transcendence of the spirit body of an individual over the physical body is becoming increasingly well recognized in the psychological and religious communities. It has especially been, and is more strongly now than ever, the conviction of those who have given serious attention to the science of mind, extrasensory perception, and the occult in religious experience. Alice was one who knew this reality.

The recognition that the natural healing processes of the human body and spirit are often preferable to the use of processes and chemicals which disrupt the normal functioning of a person is not acceptable in many quarters or by many persons. While making a commitment to all legitimate therapies of medical and psychological science, the person seeking spiritual reality must recognize increasingly the movement toward wholeness of body and spirit that is possible in submission and openness to influences and conditions which come from God and transcend the power of human capacities.   —A. D. W.

HEALTH AND SPIRITUAL ADJUSTMENT

A young mother of two children had had a rather serious health problem since the birth of the second child. She believed she could not have any more children because of certain functions no longer operative within her body, so she had begun a rather energetic college education. This took much of her time, and for some years she had put it ahead of the enjoyment of her family and her home.

She had completed her master's degree and was contemplating beginning work on her doctorate, but her health had deteriorated so much that she had little energy. She had visited her doctor again and he had run some tests. He advised her to go into a certain institute for research for more tests that would normally cost around $5,000, but since they had scientific value, would cost her nothing.

Visiting me, she stretched out her hands and said, "Would you look at my fingernails?" I was horrified at what I saw. All the cuticle around the fingernails looked as if it had been chewed and eaten with some kind of chemical. She said the condition had existed for several years. At one time a doctor had taken one of the nails completely out, but the new nail was deformed. She had suffered greatly from this treatment. I asked her if she would sit with me in the silence and join in prayer with me as I sought spiritual help and advice on what to tell her and what guidance God would offer.

During this time of silence it came very clearly that basically she was healthy. She did however have a deficiency in certain vitamins and minerals since she had not cared for her body properly or fed it the things necessary for good health. I shared this insight with her, and I also revealed that I felt if she went into the institute, the treatments and procedures they would use would be more than she could humanly stand. I expressed concern about the results of the tests on her physical body.

She asked me for advice in the right nutrients, vitamins, and minerals to take. I shared with her much of my research and the different ways that I had found for getting these vitamins into my body without having to eat an excessive amount of food. She was an apt student and eager to help to cure her condition. I also shared with her many of the wonderful aspects of her husband's personality and things that she had shut herself off from in her great desire to obtain education. I also spoke of the many things she was missing in the lives of her two young daughters, who seemed somewhat similar to my two daughters at that age. Thus, I related to her in depth.

I asked her if she would let me wash her feet and hands, which would in some manner show her not only my sincerity to help her, but also make effective my prayers for her. When she agreed, I dipped her feet into a basin of warm water and saw with surprise their blueness and lack of circulation. They responded to the washing and to the quiet, soft rubbing of the toes, and her body began to relax with a comfort and warmth she said she had not know before.

Then I took her hands into mine and very gently put them in the water. Taking each finger, I prayed, asking the Lord to bless it and to heal it, promising that we also would do everything within our power to cooperate with his healing touch. All of this moved this lovely and sensitive woman greatly. When I asked her to get vitamins A and E capsules, puncture them with a pin, and use the oil on her hands several times each day, she readily promised she would.

She not only stopped all struggle for an education, content to have her master's degree, but began to find a whole new world in the lives of her children, her husband, and her home. She began to work in her garden, to enjoy her neighbors, and for the first time in a long time she said she found herself laughing.

"I have found that my two daughters are really angels sent to me," she remarked to me one day. She also began to enjoy boating and sailing and found energy to carry out many of the activities that before she had denied herself. Very faithful in her intake of nutrients and vitamins, she followed the suggestions with care.

One day when I met her at the church, she held out her hands with great joy and said, "Oh, Alice, look. They are almost perfect now." No one could believe, unless he had seen them before, the transformation. They were lovely with shiny, healthy nails and the cuticle around them was almost perfect in its formation and in its healthy condition.

The next Christmas I received a beautiful candle holder, a little plaque of holly, and the cross that her two daughters had made for me. I deeply treasure the wooden cross her younger child made while playing with plastics. She sent it to me along with a printed note of what the symbols on the cross meant. This is what she said:

"Title: The Meaning of This Cross. The ruby and diamond at the top and bottom stand for all the jewels in the world which added together would equal far less than the crown in the middle which stands for God. The blue piece on one side of the cross stands for sadness which God helps you get over. The yellow piece on the other side stands for gladness, sunshine, plants, and life, and the cross itself stands for Jesus Christ our Saviour. Love, Christine."

When real spiritual healing comes to a home or to a family, it does not come to one member alone, but its pervasive spirit spreads out into the lives of all living there. Such healing had happened in this family, as expressed in the words written by a child who received spiritual understanding that has been a blessing to her family and to her playmates.

The now healthy woman has grown in her prayer life in a remarkable way and has been able to influence her husband so that they began to keep a daily prayer vigil in their home and have both grown in their Christian expression and work in the church.

A HEALING OF
A VISITOR FROM OVERSEAS

One day in Washington after I spoke at a meeting, a lady from the Diplomatic Corps approached me and asked if I would drive her home. I noticed she had a lame leg, so I gladly helped her. When she got into the car, she began to tell me of her difficulties.

She had found the adjustment from their post in South Africa to America very difficult, both for herself and her young son. She had gone out ice skating a few months before, had fallen and broken her right leg. Although she felt she had had expert medical attention, the leg had not mended in the cast. Subsequent operations only seemed to increase the difficulty with the leg. It was becoming more deformed and crooked, and the incisions from the operations had not healed. Since she had to make many public appearances, this leg was not only painful but also detracted from her appearance and hindered her moving about.

She had become very despondent about this, and she did not know where to go and what to do further to alleviate her difficulty. She felt an act of God had brought her to the meeting that day where she heard my message of hope. When we arrived at her home, she invited me in for a cup of tea. I gladly accepted since it provided an opportunity to talk further about prayer and the guidance that she needed to know how to proceed intelligently with the help she apparently needed.

She resonded to our conversation and asked if I would especially pray for her. She said she would also willingly spend time in prayer and would remain open to guidance that would come. Upon my request, prayer partners in different parts of the world started to pray for her. Before many days had passed, she found a new doctor, and hope and light began to penetrate the dark areas of her life. The power of love began to manifest itself. When she again went to the hospital for surgery, she was open and responsive to all that medical technology could do for her. The power of prayer that surrounded her also upheld and transformed her in spirit.

Although I did not call the Embassy or make any move toward personal contact with her, I had requested that I be informed of the time of the operation. But I had not had any news from her. One Monday morning I stood in my kitchen washing my dishes when I became aware of a person standing beside me. When I turned, I knew it was a woman in the Spirit. I recognized her because she had the same features as this lady whom I had met. I received the message that this woman would go into surgery at 9 o'clock that morning for a further operation on her leg. This spirit person asked if I would especially pray for success in the operation, for complete healing of the leg.

When the vision vanished, I sat down for awhile in prayer. Then I called my husband and told him what had happened, and the time it occurred. I then sent a message of cheer and hope and good will to the hospital where I knew this lady would be, putting on it both the time and the date. She found this message waiting for her when she returned to her room after the operation was completed. It gave her such a spirit of encouragement and love that she said she showed it to her doctors and nurses and told them that they had great spiritual guidance and help during the surgery. She knew that everything now was going to be all right. She later wrote to me: "This is turning out to be a very different and a very wonderful experience. The memory of this is one that I shall gladly carry with me all my life."

The operation did prove highly successful. Her leg returned to its normal shape, the scar in time completely healed. She was able to travel and again take on speaking engagements. She conducted her life with freedom and ease, with a sense of the tremendous power of prayer in her life and the love of people whom she had not known before.

During lunch with her one day, she asked if I would tell her how I had known of the date and time of her operation, because she had neglected to inform me. I told her about the lady who had appeared in my kitchen and as I described this person, her eyes became wide with amazement. "That is my mother, but she has been dead for several years," she said. "How could you have seen her?"

I explained to her that her mother lived in the Spirit and I believe she had brought her to the meeting at which I spoke. She also had surrounded her with praying friends during these weeks and months. Furthermore, I told her that I learned her mother was a woman of great spiritual power and that while she lived on earth she had done a great deal of work with other people and had drawn to herself much love and goodwill.

She replied, "Yes, my mother was a very spiritual woman. Although she had means, she went into the different tribes, teaching them the Bible. In fact a memorial to her stands in South Africa in a church for which she helped raise funds. When she died, the people collected enough money to build an altar to her memory in the church."

This experience attests to the fact that we are part of one another, that there is no death, that when we live in the Spirit, we live forevermore, and that healing flows through all who are open to receive it.

HEALING IN A MINISTER'S FAMILY

A minister friend of ours called one day and began his conversation with the remark: "I've always been interested in spiritual healing and intended to do something about it, at least to begin to get myself informed about what's involved in spiritual healing and the power of prayer in relation to healing. But I've been so busy that I've neglected it. Now my wife has had two abdominal operations, is facing a third, and the doctors aren't giving us much encouragement. She's very depressed, and she even feels that she'd rather die than go through continued surgery."

The operation was scheduled for about two weeks later, so he had time to begin to read and get somewhat informed. I asked him whether, if I were to loan him some books, he would at least read. He readily agreed, came and took some books home. I knew if I could strike a chord in this man, I would have a much greater avenue of help to his wife. She was at this point dependent upon him and would listen to him, believe in him, and act upon his belief. I did not feel very much response to my prayers for her during these weeks. It seemed as though she kept herself in rigid tension and in fear of the impending operation.

However, he quickly grasped the meaning of spiritual healing. He responded in a magnificent way, and I felt his response and closeness in prayer as I shared it with him and for his wife. The morning of the operation came and I kept that time in silence for this woman. I did not feel a sense of peace or relaxation until I had the distinct impression that she had lost consciousness under the anesthesia. I then felt the freedom of the Spirit and a lifting and a great surge of vitality and strength flowing through me toward this woman. I knew that the love of God was moving through her being, that a change would occur in the strain and the tension of her body, that the doctor could perform the operation successfully.

Here is what the doctor said after surgery when he came to share the experience with the waiting husband: "When I looked at those muscles, separated as they were, I did not see how I could ever get them together and make them stay if I did. But there was a complete absence of tension. They were fully relaxed so that I was able to pull them together and fasten them. If there had been tension there, it might have been impossible to fasten them. If I had been able to fasten them in spite of the tension, a cough or a sneeze could have popped them apart like a tightly drawn violin string when it is cut. This has been one of the most satisfactory operations of its kind that I have ever taken part in."

This woman went on to know healing, and has enjoyed good health in all the succeeding years that I have known her.

AN ORGANIST IS HEALED

One night while visiting in another city, I was asked to take part in a healing service in one of our churches. As I spoke in the service, I turned and looked over toward the organist and immediately had the impression that I was viewing one of the ugliest men I had ever seen in my life. I thought of the healing service to follow in which I had been requested to help in the laying-on-of-hands service.

"Whatever will I do if this man should ask me to lay hands on him?" I thought. I surely would not want to touch him; actually, I felt repulsed by his appearance.

The service continued and people came to the altar for the laying-on-of-hands. As I moved among the people, I felt a shock as I found myself standing before this very man as he knelt in front of me. He lifted up his face, his eyes looked into mine, and he said, "Will you pray for me? I have just been told today that I have cancer of the throat."

A power came over me that suddenly washed away all those terrible feelings I had. I no longer saw the man in his ugly form

70

or his unpleasant face, but I saw a soul in need. I felt a flow of living water almost pouring through me. I took this man's head in my hands, cradled it against me, and began to pray with a power not mine.

A great blessing poured forth, not only for him, but when it came through me, it cleansed me also. A wonderful glow and warmth passed between this person and myself. He left the altar with a light and a radiance around him noticeable to other people sitting in the congregation. Communicating with me later, he reported the next week he went back to his doctor to have a further examination and to set the date for surgery. They did extensive tests on him; other doctors were called in; but none could find any sign of the growth. He has, by all reports that I have had, remained in good health.

SPIRITUAL HEALING THAT BROUGHT HOPE TO PEOPLE IN DISTANT LANDS

Through an answer to a phone call I became acquainted with two missionaries from Rhodesia. A friend called as he passed through our city, asking prayer for his friend who had just arrived in New York from the mission field for a delicate eye operation. There was great fear that this man would become totally blind.

As I spoke on the phone about the seriousness of the eye condition, I had a vision of this man and said: "Your friend is Norwegian; he is fair and has clear blue eyes. I see him surrounded by many good forces. Call them the communion of saints, if you wish. I am being told that you must start now to relinquish this intense fear you have for his blindness because they are going to need you very much as a contact person in this country. At present you are only picking up and intensifying their fears. We will pray for him but help must come to his wife also or she will become a prisoner of the blindness herself."

He promised to carry out some specific instructions as I assured him of my prayers. Immediately in praying for the missionary I felt a contact with spirit bodies, people who loved him and felt concern for his welfare.

Praying for the first operation as it approached, I received insight into this man's subconscious mind. I seemed to move through a picture gallery. At one picture, of his mother who was totally blind, I stopped. Further pictures told of his deep love for the mother, of his inner distress at the time of her blindness, and of his sincere desire to make an atonement to her even to his willingness to go to the mission field and to give himself for others. I also learned of his obsession with his own eyes. He sometimes used furloughs for eye examinations and much of their concern as a family revolved around his eyesight. Now he had almost lost the sight in the one eye and the other was dimming.

The best surgeon for such an eye operation was obtained. He also understood prayer and the effect of inner tensions upon such surgery.

One day a letter came from the missionary's wife thanking me for my prayers. She ended it by telling me of the many people praying for her husband. In the final sentence she wrote, "And of course his blind mother in Norway." This gave me the opening I needed to contact her by phone and ask about his attitude toward the mother. She told me that this had been a closed subject, one she could not mention to her husband or anyone else. She expressed a great relief to have someone with whom to share her thoughts.

A few nights later the mutual friend who had first called me, and who, as their superior in the mission board for many years, had visited them many times at the mission school, came to my home for dinner. Our conversation turned to his friend and I told him of my talk with the wife and said that unless something could be done about the image he had, the doctor worked against great odds.

My guest inquired about what image I spoke. Assuming he knew, I replied, "That of his blind mother."

Startled, he exclaimed, "I never knew he had a blind mother and I have been his closest friend all these years." Together we remembered the scripture, "The thing I feared has come upon me."

Though not able to change the picture in his friend's mind, our friend did become a mediating counsellor between the patient and his wife. A healing process began that had far reaching effects. The man agreed for the first time to good counselling help. Though almost totally blind, he, together with his wife, became a student of Braille. He learned to use a seeing-eye dog and could move around quite freely. He went to various national meetings and presented his work with poise and wisdom. Later in the year he and his wife spent the summer at his home in Norway.

After a time I received letters telling of the deep healing in the family situation and of the new freedom with which they could now enjoy life. Their prayers were answered when the Mission Board reassigned them to teaching positions on the field. They went back with an added skill and understanding for many of the blind people in their part of Rhodesia. For example, they could now teach the blind to read and write. This opened to them a beautiful new field of service with many wonderful people who before had no hope.

A REVELATION OF A FUTURE HEALING

During my period of deep meditation one morning in our library, the appearance of the person of Jesus Christ came to me. He held in his hands a heart, a live, functioning, throbbing organism. I asked why he showed me this, and Christ replied it was the heart of a certain man whom I had known in our work in the church over many years, but not as a personal friend to myself. I had not seen or had contact with this person for several years.

Now I saw his heart, and the exact intricate part needing healing. The Spirit said, "I must heal this heart," and I knew within that I would be part of the healing. A considerable time passed in the Spirit when I became caught up completely in the work of this mission. At the time of such an experience, I lose all sense of timing and space; all is Spirit and I am conscious of nothing else.

After awhile I returned to consciousness and rested on the floor for a period. Later that morning I went into the basement to put a wash into the machine when the phone rang. "Alice Ward, this is. . . . I am sitting in my office in New York and an overwhelming urgency that I must call you now came over me."

I told him that I knew what had happened and related in detail the story of the past hour. He was astounded, saying, "But no one knows about this except my heart specialist and myself, not even my wife!"

I replied, "But the Lord knows and he had heard your prayer and chose to use me as the one person in answering your prayer."

Then I was able to help him see and rethink a series of events he had passed through a short time before. He began to realize how the effects of these were adversely affecting the heart circulation and aggravating the present condition. He also saw many of the factors and people involved in a new light as knowledge came from the spirit mind to illumine his. Rather than worrying only about the effects, we talked about the cause that created (and was continuing to create) the situation bringing about his heart condition.

This man knew I had no way of gaining this information about him or his affairs, and he believed the spirit of God in love had truly reached through to answer his prayers.

In the following years he has known increasing freedom both within himself and without. He has traveled all over the world in his great work for others and enjoyed increased health and vitality. He knows with surety the goodness of God, as it continued to work deep in his subconscious mind, releasing him.

I learned through prayer that he carried a fear created in early childhood. I wrote describing the outer manifestations of this fear that had plagued him all his growing and adult life, though he could not discern its roots. Now the picture became very clear and he could understand. A series of events followed, some very challenging, and because he now knew and partially understood the forces at work, he could change his approach in many cases. Thus, the picture became new, with his fear transmuted into faith. Not just a case of treating the defect, the understanding alleviated the basic cause and set this man free. Christ always heals that way.

A HEALING OF A RELATIONSHIP

A lady known internationally as a missionary and a writer of religious books visited a friend in Washington in preparation for a series of speaking engagements in this country and Canada. When she became ill with a blood condition, I received a request to pray especially for her. During one of my periods of meditation for her, I saw a vision which repeated itself several times and became so vivid that I related the message to her.

I saw on one hand a figure resembling a dragon about to devour her. This, I was told, represented all the big speaking engagements for which she was booked. These would literally consume her because of her physical condition and the uncontrolled demands of the people.

Then an English scene appeared before me. A path led up to a gate that stood out in detail even to the angle at which it opened. Inside the yard I saw quite a large typically English home, and some distance from it stood a relatively new, modern trailer that appeared as a guest house.

The picture remained the same in all details until a woman walked across the yard toward the gate. She showed much goodwill, almost excitement, as she began to open the gate to the person coming up the path. I saw the person approaching, a large lady in her early sixties, for whom I had been asked to pray.

The woman inside the gate appeared some years younger, but I received a very strong impression that she was in some way the mother of the older woman. I watched as many things— misunderstandings, hurts, bitterness—that had accumulated through the years began to dissolve at the very moment the gate opened, and they moved toward one another in an expression of love.

I relayed this message to the hostess of the lady whom I had not in any way known personally. When the hostess took it to her she immediately went to her room and spent the next few days almost entirely alone. Then she told her hostess that she had had guidance, and all that I had seen in prayer was true. Her real mother had died when she was on the mission field and her father later married a much younger woman who had worked in their home. Hurt by this, she had not gone back to her home all these years although her father had died and his second wife now lived there alone.

She spoke of this deep disturbance that she tried to hide by her work in prayer and religion. Now she decided to go home. She wired this woman asking permission to visit her in their home again. A reply came back, warm and inviting.

Soon she boarded a flight across the ocean. Subsequent letters, that I was permitted to read, told of the exact detail of the vision given that resulted in her complete return to health. They reported that she set up her own place for study and writing in the trailer. Most of all she found in her father's second wife a real friend and "mother image" that she very much needed for her life to become whole again.

VI

OF THINGS TO COME—CLAIRVOYANCE

INTRODUCTION

One of the areas which causes difficulty for church people, but also excites tremendous interest, is the capacity that some persons seem to possess of anticipating future events.

This is a different phenomenon from visions or revelation, because the clairvoyant person has a special capacity and through its use can pinpoint persons, times, places, and sequence of events. An additional factor is that the power does not depend on religious commitment or experience. It is very much like the "odic" healing power, which some people have, that has nothing necessarily to do with religious faith, and is the concentration of power (electrical energy might be the best analogy) in a person transmitted to others with a resulting surge of energy producing healing effects.

However, in both cases, when the capacity resides in a person with deep and growing religious commitment, the use of the power is generally highly disciplined, nonexploitive, and responsibly used. The main thrust becomes the use of the power for the service of God and of other persons without any direct anticipation of personal benefit.

Many persons with clairvoyant powers recognize certain indications within themselves, but are often apprehensive to let them be known, to utilize them, or to seek their further expression. This should not be the case, especially for a disciplined religious person who dedicates all of life and special capacities to the direction of the Holy Spirit. One should seek with confidence both the development and use of such gifts. Properly used, such powers can be of tremendous good to others and can supplement greatly the richness of one's own spiritual life.

The illustrations given here vary. Some lent themselves to immediate use. In other instances the circumstances made it difficult, if not impossible, to utilize the knowledge to affect the course of events. In one or two cases, it was apparent that to try to confront the situation would not have been very helpful. Obviously one should exercise a high degree of discrimination in the development and use of such powers.   —A. D. W.

JOHN F. KENNEDY

In the summer before the death of John Kennedy, I first saw a dark funnel in the sky. It took shape something like a whirling gray mass gathering in the sky, and then it formed into a funnel pointing down toward the earth. I saw it only for a brief time before it disappeared.

In the months that followed, as tensions and feelings increased in the country, I saw the same sign in the sky several times. Gradually, I became aware of its significance. I knew for about six weeks before the tragic event took place in Dallas that our President's life was in great danger and that he should be very careful in going into areas where the earth consciousness was heavy with hate and bitterness.

My husband went to a conference in Europe during October. As November drew nearer, I knew the time, place, and manner in which our President would meet his death. How many times I longed to have someone to talk with, but I knew from experience no one would listen to a housewife, possibly not even my own husband.

Facing this fact and relinquishing my anxiety and urge to do something, I felt that all I could do was to try to influence Dudley to be in Washington on that Friday. When I made inquiries, I found that he planned to be in Toronto, Canada flying up the night before. I used every persuasion I could think to try to make him change his plans, but to no avail.

He had a seven o'clock flight to New York but did not want to leave without saying goodbye to his young son. However, we could not find John. We searched for him and the time of departure passed. Finally we found him hiding under the guest room bed, a very strange action for him. But he had too sensed my feelings and he told his father that Mother was right, he should not go away.

When John finally went to sleep, my husband again picked

up his bags to leave. By then I knew that I should not say one word to stop him, so bid him goodbye as he went out the door that Thursday night. Through the long night I waited for the dawn which came foggy and rainy in Washington.

During all these weeks that I knew of this terrible event that would have such a far reaching effect, I kept hearing those dreadful shots, and could not even reach the one closest to me. So I did what I had been doing daily. I prayed.

At about 7:30 A.M. the phone rang and I heard Dudley say, "I am coming home, this day has never been right." When he arrived, he came in, changed his clothes and went out to dig up the dahlia roots. I kept the radio on and just did odd jobs around the house. He went down to the store and at that time the news came over the wires. When he returned, he looked at me and said, "How long have you known?" Then, for the first time, I could tell the story, even of how last night I had to let him go.

The phone began to ring. People wanted to reach Dudley for a statement from our church and the first one made came from the Board of Christian Social Concerns. Dudley was here to give to others the leadership they needed at such a time of crisis.

Again one Saturday evening the first part of June, 1968, my husband was sitting on the porch just outside the dining room. I was writing at the dining room table when he called me to come and see the face he detected forming in the sky. It was in the west and one could clearly see the outlines of a face, but the features were not too distinct. Gradually as we watched they began to come toward us and finally stood out in sharp relief against the sky.

The head even turned to show the full face and profile so one could not be mistaken. We exclaimed, "It's the face of Jack Kennedy." It was so close to us and seemed to be saying something. Only gradually did the face recede and become part of the very unusual cloud formation. I knew that he had said a name three times and that it was a warning message. A couple of weeks later Bobby Kennedy was shot to death in Los Angeles.

A BUSINESS ASSOCIATE

A man with whom my husband had been associated in business, and who was a friend over many years, had reached his seventies. Although he had great wealth and much of this world's goods, he had found little if any peace in life. This became accentuated with the limitation brought on by age itself. He seemed to show signs of losing any zest for life and a futility set in.

One night as I was kneeling before the altar in prayer, I was surprised to see this man standing "out of his body" before me. I knew as I looked that this man had either taken his own life or he had resolved to do so in his own mind and that it was just a matter of where and when the act would occur. For all intents and purposes the suicide already had taken place.

When we returned home the phone rang. It was this man calling from his home in Florida. My husband talked with him for awhile and then came to me with a strange look on his face. "Alice, I believe he will die or commit suicide. This is the last time I will talk to him. Do you think I should go to him?"

I told him what I had seen and knew. "Even if you were to go and sit with him day and night, you could not change the course of events." Although his wife and servants were in the home, within a few days he would carry out his plans. Before the end of the week he had shot himself in the head.

DEATH OF MY BROTHER-IN-LAW

While spending a few days with my family in Canada, I visited in the lovely home of my youngest sister and her husband. My brother-in-law, a handsome man with a fine physique, very strong and healthy, had done well in his contracting business. Summer months were his busiest period.

A strange knowledge began to form within me, though it was so incredible and frightening to my mind that I kept thrusting it from me. I left my sister's home and went to stay for awhile with one of my brothers, but this feeling did not leave. I knew if I mentioned this frightening knowledge to anyone, they would immediately think I had lost my senses.

I knew that my brother-in-law would be killed within a month. I left my home and family with this inner burden, trying in every way to cast it from me. When I came home I did not tell my husband the knowledge specifically, but I did insist that we had to relinquish certain responsibilities since our time and attention would be required for a pending event. Convinced by my words, Dudley changed some of his plans and shifted others, freeing a large section of his schedule.

One Sunday afternoon a month later we had just come in the door from a weekend at the ocean when we heard the phone ringing. The news I had feared had come. My brother-in-law had taken a new business associate up in his plane to look over some of the work from the air. A few minutes after takeoff the plane plunged into the bay killing both the occupants.

We left for Canada. Following the funeral we helped with the immediate necessity to see that all the construction jobs moved ahead as planned. Some were government contracts and could not be held up. Along with this, many legal and accounting problems faced the estate and my sister. Because of the schedule changes, my husband was able to stay and to give invaluable help.

I often wonder why these things are made known when seemingly there is little that can be done to change the course of events, largely because people do not accept spiritual guidance which comes through certain individuals. But I have found that, asking what I am to do personally, I always receive practical guidance and in the time of crisis am able to move so that the effect is lessened and help is often available. Often the knowledge helps us find a way to move constructively through the situation.

A HOUSE BREAKIN

We had just pulled into the driveway from a family trip to New England, when our neighbor rushed over to tell us that someone had broken into our home the night before. The intruder had entered through a lower window, after damaging one of the doors. He had not vandalized the house, and, except for peculiar signs left in certain rooms, it seemed a minor thing, though he had taken some money.

A peculiar and disturbing sign from the intruder was a number of long, burnt out matches placed among the personal clothing of my daughter. When my eldest daughter prepared to leave for college the next day, she discovered the picture she had of her younger sister was no longer there. It had been taken.

The family tended to treat the whole thing as a joke and pass it off lightly. I felt otherwise and wanted to have all the locks on the house changed because I believed the person had taken a key to the house. The family maintained that it had been taken by Dianne when she went to college.

Weeks went by, yet my anxiety increased for the safety of my younger daughter. It seemed as though at times when I had been out of the house someone had been in it. When we received the check covering the damages on the first breakin, I pleaded with my husband to change the locks. By then he was fully fed up with my premonitions of danger lurking near our daughter and our home. I knew that I had to use other tactics. So I began to pray specifically in my daughter's room each day, and often in each room of the entire house, for spiritual guidance and protection.

During one entire week late in October, I felt a force pressing against me, intensifying inside the house. When I went into my daughter's room for prayer, I saw a funnel, dark gray in color, gathering up at the ceiling and coming down to a point in the center of the room. Instinctively I knew it was a sign of impending danger.

A few friends who came for tea that day joined me in specific prayer for protection. My husband came home from a few days of travel and took our young son to a scout meeting and my daughter went out to a party. I continued my prayer vigil. Our son brought a scout friend home to sleep with him in the recreation room. By ten o'clock everyone was home and the last words my husband said to me were, "They're all settled down now and safe at home."

Later we awoke hearing a loud moan from our daughter. Dudley turned on the light and jumped out of bed, only to hear heavy steps going down the stairway, the slam of the front door, and the never-to-be-forgotten staccato sound of heels hitting the pavement as the person fled into the night. Dudley pursued the running person but never did get really close to him.

I ran to my daughter's room immediately. She sat up in bed. "Mother, I have been hit." I saw her swollen and bleeding mouth and eyes. Instinctively, I put my hands on her face and felt a warm glow underneath them. She said, "I moaned when I thought a huge truck had rolled over my head." By then her father had given up the chase, returned to the house, wondering what had actually happened to his daughter. We called the police, who searched, but found no trace of the person.

For many weeks at the exact hour of two o'clock I found myself sitting upright in bed. We had had the locks changed and precautions taken to insure the safety of the home. I drove my daughter back and forth to school and tried to take no chances for her safety. Along with my husband we began to use the hour of 2:00 A.M. for specific prayers. We prayed for the person who must have been in her room for sometime and who had with him things by which he could have beaten her unmercifully, and certainly could have committed a crime against her person. We were grateful for the fact that none of these possibilities had happened. We prayed for the healing of any damage done to our daughter's deep consciousness and for the guidance to help her when these events became active in her conscious mind.

We soon realized, as in so many such cases, that changes are often necessary. She transferred to an all girls' school where she completed her high school education. She began to discipline herself for a new kind of pattern in her relationships and she developed a wonderfully gracious, yet defensive stance in her living which led to a beautiful release from the whole ghastly experience.

JOHN AND THE CAR

One morning our young son asked permission to use the car to drive to school since he wished to stay later and attend a game. His school was some distance away from our home and meant about a half-hour drive. As he prepared to leave, I felt like telling him, "John, be extra careful when driving past school zones; they are really strict in Virginia." But I decided I had better keep my warning to myself since we had harped a bit on the need for him to watch the speed limits.

I finished the breakfast dishes and was ironing some of his clothes when I saw an event. He had been stopped by a policeman and given a ticket for speeding, a very minor offense. I finished ironing his blue shirt and hung it over the back of a chair, and had started to press his pants when the phone rang. It was John telling me that I was not to worry.

He had gotten a ticket, but it was for a small offense. He had stopped for a milk shake, turned into a school zone where there was no sign but where police had set up radar, and had driven twenty-five miles in a fifteen mile zone. When he came home, John said, "I called you because I knew you would know. I saw my blue shirt hanging over the chair and knew you were ironing my pants. So I knew that if I could see that, you also had seen what had happened to me. You know I could have told you this morning before I left this was going to happen to me but I couldn't figure out how because I tried to be extra careful."

He had to go to court and pay the fine after developing with his father an exact reproduction of the zoned area which clearly indicated no adequate warnings. (Even the police admitted this.) This all served as a lesson and has made him very conscious of speed limits and enlivened his sensitivity to a policeman or radar when driving.

A PLANE CRASH

The telephone rang. A guarded voice made inquiries about the whereabouts of A. Dudley Ward. Had he left Chicago for New York that evening? Had he planned on chairing the meeting in New York on the following day? Had I heard the news on the radio? He asked all of these and more before I could tell him my husband was at home. He had made other arrangements for the meetings in New York.

Then we heard that the plane carrying three ministerial colleagues from a meeting in Chicago to the meeting in New York had crashed at LaGuardia Airport with a total loss of life. Dudley's name was included on the passenger list. So the phone rang on!

The previous evening Dudley had come home with a clipping from the newspaper, announcing the flight of the new Electra from Chicago to New York. "Thought you would like to see the plane I will be flying on tomorrow night," he told me. I was accustomed to his travel, almost 80 per cent of the time in his particular work, but something happened as I looked at that page of newsprint.

In bold black print across the wingspread of that plane I saw the word "Death." I was so inwardly shaken that I remained speechless for sometime. I knew I had seen it, and there was no mistake about that in my mind. But I also knew my husband would just brush such a thing aside as nonsense and make doubly sure he was on that plane.

I asked for guidance. One goes through a great struggle realizing that lives are in danger and recognizing one's lack of power to communicate even to the one closest to you.

Since I had been seriously ill for several weeks and had at no time requested him to curtail his travel, I went up to the room where he was working prior to going to the office. I asked if he would phone the co-chairman in Dallas, Texas, to see if he could go to New York to chair the meeting on the following day. Perhaps it was his surprise at my making a request, but without any question, he put in the phone call, got an immediate affirmative response and left saying, "Well, guess I'll be home for dinner." I continued to agonize in prayer for those others whom I had no way of helping.

Not until Dudley had passed through some of the shock of the loss of three of his friends and colleagues, did he question me about his own decision. It was then I told him what I had seen and knew. Probably this event, more than any other, helped him to realize that there is a way of knowing events other than just through the intellect or by natural means.

A VISIT TO WASHINGTON, D. C.

Another time that I was aware of an impending event occurred one morning when I was setting my hair. Suddenly I knew that the phone was going to ring within the next five minutes and it would be Dudley calling me from Washington, D. C. He had flown from our home in Wilmette, Illinois, that morning for a meeting with Bishop G. Bromley Oxnam. So strong was this feeling that I couldn't lift my arms to finish pinning up my hair, and just had to sit there and wait.

The phone rang at the exact time, and Dudley's voice answered and I told him of knowing that he would call. He said, "That is strange because I came out of the Bishop's office and hailed a cab. The first thing I said to the driver was, "Take me to a phone booth, I must call my wife.' Ordinarily, I would wait to call you from the airport but I felt compelled to get to a phone booth right away."

He, too, seemed amazed at the synchronization of the timing. There was no other urgent reason for the call, simply a desire to share the details of the visit with the Bishop and to express in words, love and happiness. It served to increase our interest in such happenings and to demonstrate the oneness of all things.

A PROPOSED TRIP

Just after our New Year celebration I was dismantling the Christmas tree, sitting on the floor once more wrapping the balls for storage and remembering all the happy times we had had together. As I picked up a clear silver one and held it in my hands to wrap, I suddenly saw the world globe.

Fascinated by what I saw, the knowledge came to me that a friend of ours was planning a world tour and many people were going with him. I learned that he would be wise to cancel his plans now, early in the year, because he had a health situation that, while not giving him any particular discomfort at this time, would be aggravated into a problem through the strain of this travel.

When the opportunity occurred, and, in company with my husband, I felt guided to give to him the details of what I had seen and received. I knew immediately it was not welcome news and he would not listen to it. For the first time we heard of his summer plans to take a large group of people to the Holy Land and then on around the world. I felt his displeasure at what I had told him. He showed it in various ways.

One day when I was in his office, he drew my attention to a beautiful painting of the Mediterranean Sea with the remark, "When I set foot on those shores, I will know perfect health and be full of energy." I agreed it would be pleasant therapy, but felt he would be wise to listen to the guidance given, for the Mediterranean had no power in itself to heal. I suggested God was not in any way trying to restrict his freedom, but only in giving this knowledge to me was trying to save him from what seemed unnecessary suffering and time away from his work. However, he was adamant and soon left with his entire family plus sixty tourists on the world venture.

Handling this many people plus the added responsibility of teaching and speaking proved to be quite a burden for him. Less than a week after his return he went into the hospital for a condition most people attributed to the strain of the trip and change in diet. It required almost a month of recuperation at one of the busiest times of the work year.

VII
BEYOND OUR LIMITS

INTRODUCTION

One of the convictions that grew during the new experiences in our search for reality in prayer and the movement of the Holy Spirit, was that there are ways of knowing that are quite beyond the limits of our intellectual capacities and normal thought and feeling patterns. Except in limited ways and groups, the church—both its leaders and members—has hesitated and generally stridently opposed delving into such possibilities. Thus, fringe movements, the occult groups, the sensationalists, and often the exploiters have had this entire area of inquiry and experience to themselves.

Now the church is looking more rationally at this situation as the physical and psychological sciences have begun to reveal insights, data, and conclusions giving support to assumptions and experiences very much a part of the biblical record and both Jewish and Christian traditions.

The events in this chapter may seem unusual, if not unbelievable, to most people, in or out of the church. While I can make no claim to understand or to explain the details of such phenomena as astral travel, extrasensory perception, unusual symbolism, I do know enough of the details of these experiences, the people involved, and the accuracy of the descriptions to be confident that these are genuine events. They fit with our basic assumptions which grew over the years that the unusual can happen. As a matter of fact, I now can no longer close my mind or emotions to the unlimited possibilities of spiritual experience.

I hope that these experiences may prompt many to explore the wider ranges of their own spiritual development with assurance and excitement.

—A. D. W.

ASTRAL TRAVEL—
REENERGIZING OF ANOTHER PERSON

Dawn had just broken into our bedroom on this June morning of 1958, in Wilmette, Illinois. As I gradually awakened with the light, I grew aware of a need coming to me from my husband who had flown to the east coast to address a conference in the New England states.

As the vividness of this need grew, I became aware of a presence in the room with me and of a voice telling me of his exhaustion. I replied by saying that if I knew where he was I would send him energy and love through the power of prayer.

The answer came back: "There is no mystery there. All this is known to Spirit. Give your consent to the spirit person within your physical body to go to him and I will take you there."

I gave my consent but said, "Not in this blue nightgown." As at other times, I followed the same methodical procedure in choosing from the clothes on the hangers the right color to blend with the summer days. In this case I chose a blue cotton dress and when I was ready, I was told that Dudley, very tired the night before, had left the conference and had come down to Boston. He was in a hotel and I saw the room number clearly on his door.

Time lapses as one moves through space and comes to the place of descent to the earth atmosphere. It is similar to moving from a rarified atmosphere in which you move and breathe with ease to a denser, more difficult one that slows movement. You do everything in order, entering a hotel and going up the elevator to the room, and yet moving through everything because there are no barriers. You see the people but know they are unaware of you.

When I came into Dudley's room I immediately blended with the color vibration and saw him lying on the bed in an exhausted sleep. As the vibrations moved out from me they raised the level of those in the room until they reached a certain level. I stood in the center of the room, at no time moving near to his person or changing my position. All the action was taking place within me and moving out like rays of electricity or light beams, energizing everything because all was one.

When the desired level had been realized, my mission was complete and I returned in the same way and in identical order in which I had gone. At no time in this astral journey did I have a sense of being alone. Always I had guides with me and

I felt secure. Eventually I became aware of being back in my physical body. The reality of the event became more real each hour as I awaited news from Dudley.

Toward evening a cab drove up and we were all delighted to see that he was home. Later that night as we were sitting alone on the porch, he began to tell me of the events. It was for me like hearing a record to the minutest detail. His exhaustion, his desire to get to Boston to be on hand for an 8:00 A.M. appointment Sunday morning, and the difficulty in finding a hotel room. Finally after securing one at the Statler, the decision not to call me at that hour and the apprehension that came over him when he finally did lie down, realizing his intense tiredness, yet unable to sleep. Toward morning his restlessness finally gave way to an incredible peace and he fell into a deep sleep, so deep that he did not hear his alarm and only the incessant ringing of the phone aroused him.

For a few moments, he could not make contact with the outer world, then it came quickly, and his body responded with an energy and vitality that made it possible for him to be in the lobby in record time greeting his appointment. Not only was his body revitalized, but his mind provided all the details and information that he needed to make the interview quickly and successfully.

Then he looked at me and said, "Alice, you came to that room because I saw you."

I said, "If you saw me, tell me what I had on."

"You had on your blue cotton dress and you stood in the center of the room with light radiating from you. That is when I fell into the deep sleep." We went to our bedroom cupboard and he pulled out the blue cotton dress I had worn. Then I showed him the notes I had made early that morning which verified all he had just told me.

ASTRAL TRAVEL—
A VISIT TO LINCOLN, NEBRASKA

Another time when Dudley had flown out to Lincoln, Nebraska, to speak at the college there, another astral travel event happened. He had made no previous reservation, expecting local people to care for him. But arriving late at night he found no arrangements had been made. Since this was also a time of great physical strain, he wondered what to do. He called a friend who said he knew a lady with an apartment in her home and she offered her place for the night. He knew that I would be asleep in our home in Washington, D. C. so did not phone me to let me know where he was staying.

During the night I became conscious of his deep state of exhaustion and expressed my willingness to help if I knew where he was. Again the Spirit responded with the information to the minutest detail, the only requirement made of me was my consent to be the vehicle of grace. I carefully chose the dress I would wear, a white silk with a black pattern in it, to blend perfectly with the decor.

The presence informed me of Dudley's need to find a place and of the kind woman. I asked about entering a private home but was told not to be concerned. Dudley slept in a guest room added on to the side of the house, with its own private entrance, and I saw the steps leading up to the entrance. Once everything was revealed and preparations for the astral journey made, we began our trip.

In this state I was conscious of moving close to the earth's atmosphere but could sometimes see things as though moving through the air in a plane. The guide told me the area I was moving over, and it seemed as normal and real as airplane travel has become. When we arrived at the place, I felt a gradual descent into the heavier atmosphere.

Everything appeared as I had seen it and I understood why that particular dress. The room had white walls, black carpet, and red chairs. I stood in the center of the room and watched as the energy began to flow through me out into the atmosphere. I literally could see Dudley's body relax and take on new vitality as the life force within him was recharged. Again everything in the room was charged and it all became part of the whole.

When this had reached a certain level, I was told the mission had ended and we would return. The trip back was similar, all done in order and everything, including the dress, hung in its proper place. Then I became conscious of being once again part of the physical body, and felt peace and vitality within.

In the morning the phone rang and it was Dudley telling me of his whereabouts. During the conversation he remarked about how I would like this room. Then he paused and said, "You came here last night, I felt your presence and this morning when I awoke my strength was completely restored." I then told him about the house and the position of the guest room, the decor of the room and the graciousness of his hostess. All these facts he confirmed as true.

ASTRAL TRAVEL
THROUGH SPIRITUAL PLANES

This incident took place in January, 1958, while I was in the hospital in Chicago. In a private room, fully awake and in command of myself, I was alone in the early evening, lying on my bed with several tubes attached to my body.

I later became aware that I was out of my body, suspended in the room and looking with complete ease at my physical body lying on the bed attached to the various mechanical devices. I felt as though my physical body were a shell that had just naturally opened up and released me. This seemed very right and normal as did everything that followed.

After looking at my body for awhile, I grew aware of the lightness and freedom of movement within my present form. It was identical in appearance to the physical but was not bound by anything. For a time I stayed in the room moving freely about in any direction without being obstructed by articles of furniture or walls. I just passed through such things.

When I began to move out beyond the present surroundings. I became conscious of different planes, very marked, and I was conscious of the color tone of each one. The people living on each plane reflected the color of that particular plane, with degrees of light present there. I met many people whose faces remain as vivid to me today as they were then, all ages, all walks of life and conditions of men. The difference from one plane to another was the degree of light in consciousness.

Soon I moved quite quickly through amazing realms with

softness of air, beautiful colors, and great vitality present until I saw just ahead of me a blaze of glory, everything illuminated and bathed in a brilliant light. I seemed to sense that if I took one more step I would completely sever my connection with all that had been on earth and enter my next plane of life. At this plane a figure stood before me and I knew it was the Christ. Like scenes on a screen, the various stages of my life moved across and as each one came it was fulfilled and I spoke in gratitude for it. My youth and the family, the growing up years, education, romance, marriage, children, the opportunities for service and travel.

As I looked out upon this panorama, it all seemed complete and there was nothing that I desired in the earth world. I did not want to go back and requested of the Lord that I be permitted to enter eternity, to take that next step. It was then he spoke to me: "Alice, I have let you see how easy it is to leave the body and to move through the various planes if you have even a little light, but I cannot grant your request to enter into this light tonight. You are to go back into the earth world and you are to live without whimpering."

I knew the moment I had entered the body shell again and felt the limitations and pain of this human body. In the days and weeks that followed, this command came to me almost from nowhere as I faced indescribable pain. At other times it came in the middle of the night when I seemed most alone and at the point of giving in. I would see my eldest daughter, then fourteen, standing at the foot of my bed saying, "Mother, you were told not to whimper and you are getting dangerously close to doing it."

As quickly as she appeared, she would leave and in the morning she had no awareness that she had come to my room. Always, I would receive an inner strength and confirmation that enabled me to go on and in doing so not to whimper.

ASTRAL TRAVEL—
HEALING AT A DISTANCE

A one-and-a-half year old son (whom I had never seen) of a staff colleague of my husband was taken to the hospital with an unusual sound in his head, causing him to be fretful and not his usual active self. Doctors could not detect the trouble at first and were very hesitant on how to proceed. This came to my attention during a trip east from Chicago.

I was asked to pray for him, and I requested a few other persons to pray with me. We, together, kept a constant prayer vigil for the little boy.

The morning I left to return to my home in the midwest, I learned the doctors were going to do some special tests and expected to operate that afternoon. I took the bus to Friendship Airport, a ride of an hour or more. Seated on the bus, I began to pray for this child. While my physical body rode on the bus my spirit body went on a mission of healing.

I had taken great care as to the color of the dress I wore, the low heeled shoes and the neat simplicity of my appearance. I was to appear as nearly like his mother as possible. The color of the dress was a light, pinkish orange. When all was in order, I saw the hospital where he had been taken. I remember walking up to the front entrance and entering as others entered, except I moved more quickly since I confronted no barriers.

I took the elevator up to his floor and walked down the corridors to the exact room. I would know the child by the curl on his head, and all I had to do was blend so completely into the atmospheric conditions around his that I wouldn't cause the least disturbance. I would quietly place my left hand on the right side of his head back of the curl, hold it there for awhile, and then quietly leave the hospital. The Spirit did this with great order and authority. When I again became conscious of being in my body, the bus had just turned off the main highway into the terminal and I had complete command of all my natural faculties.

On Sunday morning while kneeling to receive holy communion on World-Wide Communion Sunday, a vision appeared before me. I had not heard any news from the child's family. I saw a living room and a large oval braided rug. In the middle of the rug sat the little boy with the fair curly hair, laughing at all his family standing around him—his mother, expecting her fifth child, his father and three older brothers. The room was filled with light, love, and joy, and I knew that his healing had begun and he had been returned to the center of his home and family. I received a call later that day from a friend who asked, "What happened to you at the altar today, Alice? When you turned to come down the aisle there was a light all around you."

Several months later I again traveled east and received an invitation to visit the home of this child. I wondered if everything would appear as I had seen it in the spirit.

As I walked from the car to the house the father and children came out to greet me and instantly I knew the child, even to the curl on his head. Upon entering the house, I met his mother who seemed as I had visualized her. I saw the living room was the exact room in all detail that I had seen at the altar.

A few years later this same child fell from a tree and fractured his arm. Although the doctors attempted to set the arm several times, the bone would slip out of place. Late one night the phone rang, and after I answered it I heard the voice of his father telling me of the situation and of the fact that the physicians planned to operate in the morning, and, if necessary, wire it in place.

Immediately, I knew there was no need for the procedure and assured the father that if he would yield this child into the arms of Christ and stop his anxious prayer, the arm would be set without difficulty in the morning. All through the night I held him in the healing light. The next morning the bone slipped into place and healing came quickly so that with added physical therapy and exercise he soon had full use of his arm.

This child is unusually sensitive and highly attuned to the Spirit. For such a one I find no effort in prayer, just a joy to share in the whole procedure of healing and cure for him. It is very important for the protection and development of such a soul that he be at all times surrounded by the light and daily prayed for protection from adverse energies.

THE LOVE OF GOD BREAKS THROUGH

This story began one day as I sat under the dryer in the beauty parlor. People passed in front of me and I paid little attention, feeling very relaxed. Then an inner voice said, "I want you to pray for this person."

The command came so suddenly it startled me, and when I raised the hood to look for the person, I saw the girl who had just passed. I lowered the hood and sat in contemplation. Soon I found myself agreeing for I could see she limped and had difficulty with one deformed leg. Thinking of the physical aspects, I said, "Yes, Lord, I will pray for her leg." Quickly the Spirit corrected me and said, "It is not her leg that I am asking you to pray for, but the internal condition of her soul." The Spirit assured me that she was a chosen one of God, very beautiful in her spirit but an event had happened that caused a freezing of the flow of life and love within her.

I noted that she was the manicurist and realized I had not noticed her before because I did not generally get my nails done. In the weeks before my next visit, I faithfully prayed for this person, lifting her into the area of the light. On my next visit I was guided to have my nails manicured. I saw that she wore a diamond on her engagement finger and in the course of the chitchat, I mentioned it. As she held out her hand for me to admire I saw rather than a beautiful stone radiating love, an ice machine manufacturing ice around her heart and causing a flow of tears and embarrassment.

On another visit she came and sat on a chair by me and asked if I told fortunes to which I replied, "No." She had felt a power about me and remembered me from my last visit. I told her that I prayed for people whom the Spirit asked me to pray for, or who personally requested it. She asked then if I would please pray for her and I gladly said, "Yes."

Another time as my hair was drying the Spirit said, "Write this on a piece of paper and give it to her: 'You have a sister in the city who has a safety deposit box. Take off the diamond ring and put it in this deposit box. When you have done this you can phone me and come to see me.'"

I gave the note to her as I left. She later phoned and told me she had done exactly as the note had said. One evening she came to my home and told me the story behind the ring.

She, a beautiful Greek girl from a prominent family, had fallen in love with a young American man of the Methodist Church. After they had become engaged and set the wedding date, she had enjoyed several showers and a large engagement party. A week before the wedding he phoned her to say the government was sending him on a new special job to Africa and all wedding plans were off. He insisted that she keep the ring. Her embarrassment was so great as she confronted her family and friends that she withdrew from everything, including the church.

At this time she took the job with people who knew nothing about her and kept wearing the ring in hopes he would come back. She told me that she worked her hours, went home to her apartment, and in her loneliness and bewilderment would cry until she became like ice inside. She told me that since she had taken the ring off, she was not crying as much, nor did she get the icy chills which had plagued her.

Once we sat in the silence together and prayed, I saw a vision of a young man bending over a drafting board, and I got the distinct impression that he was not in Africa, but Germany. It was in the latter part of November and he was dressed in heavy clothes with a bulky sweater. She said, "You have described him and he must have been reassigned." She obtained his new address, and since Christmas was coming, she wanted to write to him. But finally she agreed to the guidance that I should write to him for her.

This I did as a minister's wife in the church to a fellow member, telling him honestly and simply what his action had meant to this girl and asking him to release her both in his desires and thoughts. Although I did not hear from him in person, my letter was not returned and again I received confirmation of increased freedom.

The next guidance given for her was that she return to her church (Greek Orthodox) activities and friends. This really frightened her. She felt she could never go back because people would remember. When I assured her that people were too much interested in themselves to keep remembering her trouble, she agreed to go.

Her joy was wonderful to see as everyone greeted her with such love and enthusiasm, and the priest put his arms around her to show his true affection. No one mentioned her disappointment and she found her place as a person in the fellowship once more.

Each succeeding time I visited her, I saw the ice melt and dissolve in the free flowing of life. Her eyes came alive and a new beauty and color came into her face.

As I came out of a department store one day, I bumped into the woman, all radiant with the exciting news. "I have a date tonight and I am going to buy a new dress." One of the eligible young bachelors in her church fell in love with her and she with him. Before many months they became engaged and we attended their wedding in the Greek Orthodox Church. We have visited them in their home on several happy occasions, and their lives testify to the presence of God and to his guidance in their marriage and life. Before marrying, she disposed of the diamond ring, so she was free from all entanglements with the former unhappy experience.

VIII
CONCLUDING REFLECTIONS

The events in this book and their implications must stand alone and bear the scrutiny of other persons in search of a vital spiritual life. Obviously the patterns will not be the same for all, but one factor *is* essential to all: the increasing capacity for an effective prayer life, sustained meditation and silence, and the realization of strength in intercession.

To highlight some of the thoughts and the process that were part of Alice's search and achievement I compiled some of her reflections on prayer, silence, prayer groups, and healing from her copious notes:

* * * * *

Prayer groups, as such, have in no way supplanted my own personal discipline in prayer. Groups can change both in membership and purpose, or one can suddenly find himself required to move away. All these possible changes necessitate that one establishes prayer life in communion with Christ; one should seize the opportunity to share in a prayer group as the outreach of one's own prayer life. Through such groups a person grows and reaches out to help more people. Each activity becomes interdependent and interrelated to the growth necessary in prayer.

For some of the lesser needs of people I feel adequate to the prayer request, but many of the requests and burdens require sustained prayer power over a long period of time. Thus it becomes important to know other people to contact who will share effectively in the prayer need. In sudden crisis these other persons can become involved and release the maximum prayer power at that time. No matter how well-trained a person becomes in the art of prayer, all stand in need of others' prayers.

In the relationship of healing and prayer, all healing is of

God. Only as we come to him through Christ can we eventually know the true meaning of healing. Christ is concerned about our physical well-being, since a strong, healthy body is a great asset in doing service for him. However, he is not limited by a physically strong or perfect body. His power remains the same always and its fullness and perfection does not depend on our perfection. It comes always in all its fullness, wholeness, and perfection. It knows no limitations when given free access through a life wholly dedicated to him.

God's healing power regularly becomes evident through the work of skilled and dedicated physicians. The doctor who performed my operation for breast cancer helped to undergird the faith by which I lived each day in the realization that all health does come from God and that the power of love does bring healing.

Prior to my operation, I had established no basis of understanding with the doctor. When surgery became necessary, I had been referred to him, one of the top surgeons in this field, and put complete trust in his ability.

In the early dawn of a wintry Chicago, before they came to prepare me for surgery, I kept my quiet time with God. I could feel the lump in my breast. If, when I returned from the operating room to look out my bedroom window again, I saw night skies and street lights. I would know that the surgeons had performed radical surgery for cancer.

That moment came, many, many hours later. As consciousness made me aware, before I spoke to anyone, I turned my head to the window and saw the Drake Hotel outlined against the night with a blaze of electric lights.

Then the surgeon came into my room. He wore a business suit and appeared to me not only as the doctor who had performed the surgery, but also a fellowman. He came to the side of the bed and took my hand in his, holding it in a firm grip and looking directly into my eyes. His gaze remained steady, and somehow I felt strength as his hand held mine and we shared several moments of silence.

I became aware in the silence that another human being had identified himself with me in my suffering. Out of the calm that existed at the center of his being flowed a power that touched a responsive center within my being. He did not extend sympathy; rather I became aware of the compassion and love that flowed from this person, and I knew I was not alone.

Quietly, honestly, frankly he explained the operation to me, the procedure he had used and the reasons for it. He told me the tumor was cancerous and that I had had radical surgery, that I would have to take X-ray therapy treatments. All the time he talked, he never removed his eyes from mine or his hand from my hand.

The attitude and approach of this surgeon set the stage for the role into which the disease had suddenly thrust my husband and me. In the victory of the reality of those hours lay the secret and the source of strength and joy that we have found in living all the days since then.

I had known surgery before, and in my life and work as a minister's wife I had contacted other cancer patients. I had visited with them, known the stress of the family, and recognized the sometimes valiant efforts put forth to conceal the fact of the disease from the patient. Frequently the patient moved toward death in a false atmosphere with no one—doctor, family, friends, even minister—speaking honestly with him or her. Some patients even received false hopes from the others, but more often than not, they knew the truth within their hearts and also playacted.

On the other hand, I have known cases where everyone knew the truth and the family had such a dread and fear of cancer that they projected their fears into the being of the diseased person. In some cases the patient stood a chance of recovery, but knowing the constant uncertainty in the minds of those with whom he lived, he reflected their attitudes and did not regain the health possible for him. Some people conduct health-giving forces; others automatically drain the patient of his inner strength and nullify the healing forces. In one family a healing can occur; in another it may take longer, or be impossible.

The doctor should help the patient understand that although he has some knowledge in the field of cancer, he does not yet have all the answers. It will help the patient to realize the tremendous scientific and technological progress made in the tireless search for a cure for cancer. But he should also realize that still unexplored fields remain. Furthermore, he should seek to understand that those who have experienced cancer belong to the vast stream of mankind trying to find answers to many of life's unsolved questions.

My own search and my struggle with cancer—the aloneness and silence of the cobalt therapy room, the awareness of the changes that surgery had brought to my body—all had an effect on my involvement in the Ministry of Prayer and Healing.

That ministry has taken place in the silence with God. I receive a request for prayer or meet a person who communicates a need for himself or another. A letter or a phone call comes and the ministry begins again. The people for whom I pray become part of the awareness of my life and part of the God-given burden of compassion and concern for his children. In many cases I have no personal contact or I may not hear from the person for extended periods of time.

Sometimes God gives the opportunity to participate in a personal way. I continue prayer for the person as long as he remains part of the group which God has entrusted to me for prayer. Every person is part of my worldwide concern but, on this level of prayer, it seems that God gives me certain persons for whom to pray especially. Prayer for these persons never becomes a burden no matter how long I pray for them.

With the responsibility comes great joy and indwelling power. I am never allowed to neglect them or to forget to pray for them; they will come into my presence daily as the Spirit speaks to me. I am not made responsible for their healing or wholeness; that is always in the hands of God; but I am committed to daily, hourly, if necessary, offering of myself as the channel, the direct line of help to these persons. Time, space, knowledge, separateness are all dissolved in the flow of the Spirit.

Being nothing and possessing no power precludes me from making any claims or taking any praise to myself. It is Christ and he alone through whom the activity takes place. When I am permitted to visit someone, I know the presence of Christ makes the difference. To him all the praise and thanks must be given. Sometimes this power is manifested in miraculous physical healings. But always, when received with gladness, it brings renewed spiritual health and peace of body and mind. Spiritual healing goes to the root of the trouble, to the very cause, to bring about healing not alone for this life, but for all eternity.

In the identifying of the whole person into the wholeness of the Christ we become like him and then he can use us to minister to the whole of man. As the self is absorbed into the body of Christ, it takes on new life and beauty that is of God and for his glory. This new being in Christ has a transparency whereby the very breath of God breathes through it. Health and healing take place in the movements of the Spirit not only to the one through whom this power is transmitted, but to the individual, the group, the multitudes eager and willing to receive. This has been a great adventure in which I pray I can say like Paul, "Whatever gain I had, I counted as loss for the sake of Christ. Indeed I count everything as loss because of the surpassing worth of knowing Christ Jesus my Lord." (Philippians 3:7-8a.)

✿ ✿ ✿ ✿ ✿

Thus, the record stands. The ranges of spiritual experience are unlimited. Personal appropriation of the possibilities available is open to all who seek. Growth and movement toward new life in the Spirit are the most exciting of all adventures. Seek first the Kingdom of God. —A. D. W.